What Readers Said About Horse Listening: The Book

With over 20 "Five Star" ratings, *Horse Listening – The Book*, the first book in this series, has received great reader reviews and praise!

Excellent book! This is now my "go-to" book when I am not connecting with my horse. I totally get that it is typically rider error (me!) when I do not get the response I am expecting from my horse. It gives me a clearer picture in my head as to what body part I need to engage when asking the question. I have been waiting for a guide book such as this one to help me visualize lightness and balance in my riding. I can't put this book down! I carry it in my gear bag and even to work in my work bag so that I can reread certain segments of the book. – East Coast Horse Lady

Kathy Farrokhzad is a talented writer. She has a unique ability to write about dressage and horse training in general. The principles of dressage can seem very complicated and overwhelming. Kathy has a special gift in communicating the concepts clearly and logically without making it seem like rocket science. I love her Horse Listening Blog and the book is a must have for dressage riders or riders of any equine discipline who want to learn effective and humane riding techniques that can improve the human-equine relationship, be more effective in their cues and free a horse's potential for flowing and powerful movement. – Barbara

On the "must read" list for my students. Especially if you are a dressage oriented rider every page will hit home (or needs to!) Well worth the price of the book if you consider the cost of lessons and here you have reading that will sustain you for years. Can and needs to be read over and over. – Sheryl Butler

Horse Listening: Book 2

FORWARD AND ROUND TO TRAINING SUCCESS

KATHY FARROKHZAD

Photographs by Natalie Banaszak
Illustration by Jeff Thompson

A Collection of Articles From

Horse Listening: The Blog

Published by:

Full Circle Equestrian
P.O. Box 216
Ballinafad, ON, Canada N0B 1H0

www.horselistening.com

DEDICATION

For the horses who keep giving, and the riders who keep learning.

LIVING IN FLYING CHANGES

Moonless
evening darkness.
Noiseless calm-filled quiet;
even the animals are sleeping.
Horse and rider snugly enveloped in a soothing twilight
blanket
watched by twinkling diamond specks in the ever-far but
oh-so-near sky,
capably cantering.
Weightless footfalls soundlessly landing
save for the faint crunch of almost-frozen sand underfoot,
leaving large figure-eights and loops behind
as she reaches loftily ahead
in a rocking-horse rhythm,
effortlessly progressing through space and time.
Perky-eared bay mare boldly expressing her
creativity, living in flying changes.

CONTENTS

SAFETY FIRST 10

The Hind End..11

Section 1: The Theory ~ Forward & Round....................17

1 Impulsion: How Two Easy Strides of Energy Might Solve Your Horse Riding Problem...19

2 Five Components of the Ultimate Warm-Up 23

3 What Being on the Forehand Means to the Horse..........33

4 Frame, Round or Collection?..38

5 How Do You Know Your Horse is Using His Back?......43

6 Can You Accordion Your Horse? 47

7 Why Most Horses Should Slow Down and How To Do It 52

8 How to Improve the Sewing-Machine Trot 62

9 On Slobber, Snorts and Sheath Sounds 65

Section 2: The Skill ~ Rider Development.........................71

10 Riding For the Rest of Us 72

11 A Cautionary Horse Tale..75

12 Fourteen Ways to Communicate While Riding Your Horse 78

13 The Dynamic Dependency of Horseback Riding 85

14 Demystifying "Contact"..89

15   On Bubbleneck and Marshmallow Contact.................94

16   One Simple Way to Quiet Your Hands While Riding Horses 101

17   Twenty Signs That Your Horse Benefits From Your Riding..105

18   What Do Leg Aids Mean?.....................................108

19   Stop Kicking the Horse!.......................................113

20   Why Would You Bother to "Scoop" Your Seat Bones? 118

21   Move to Stay Still on Horseback...........................122

22   Living (Horse) Life in the Basics.........................126

23   Top 10 Ways to Reward the Horse 131

24   The Need for "Yes" Speed – While You Ride Your Horse...136

25   Do You Make This Timing Mistake?.....................141

26   First, Plan Your Ride. Then, Be Ready to Scrap It. 146

27   Quit to Persevere 149

28   What To Do When Your Horse Isn't Being Cute 152

Section 3: The Training ~ Getting Deeper Into The Basics 161

29   Muscle Memory Matters in Horse Riding 162

30   Blueprinting – the Good, the Bad, the Ugly 165

31   Bend: How to Drift Out on Purpose 169

32   How to "Fill Up" Your Outside Rein for a True Neck

Rein 174

33   Four Steps to Help Your Horse Through a Turn 179

34   Why You Must Shoulder-Fore Your Horse on the Rail
and How To Do It 184

35   Two Secrets to Easing Your Horse Into Suppleness ...190

36   How to "Flow" From the Trot to the Walk.................195

37   What To Do When the Half-Halt Just Won't Do.........199

38   Why a Halt is Not a Vacation 204

39   Done With Going Round and Round on the Rail? Try
the "10/5" Challenge! 209

40   Twenty-Three Ways to Solve the Riding Problem.......214

41   Finding Your Horse's "Happy Place"........................217

42   Dressage As A Healing Tool...................................225

43   Forty-Two Ways to Play, Learn and Grow With Your
Horse 229

The Front End 232

SAFETY FIRST

In all of this book's chapters, as in all riding, concern for the horse's well-being, health and longevity is at the forefront of our efforts. It is also the method behind the madness of all the suggestions contained in this book.

As with all physical endeavors, horseback riding requires a certain level of fitness, balance and coordination. The unpredictable nature of the horse always adds an element of uncertainty and danger that we need to be aware of.

Please use any and all of the suggestions in this book at your discretion. Feel free to change anything to meet the needs of you and your horse. Finally, be sure to "listen", because the horse will always let you know if you are on the right track.

The Hind End

In riding, we always start with the hind end of the horse. The key to all "good" movement (which essentially translates into healthy movement for the horse) starts with energy and impulsion – which begins in the hind end.

And so, let us begin this book with the consideration of the horse's hind end.

When I started riding dressage, I was introduced to one glaring truth that kept appearing and reappearing pretty much in every aspect of every ride. I would be working on one aspect of riding – let's say, the upward transition. To improve the transition, I discovered I needed more impulsion.

Then I worked on the downward transition. Although I felt that I was getting a fairly crisp and responsive transition, I found out that there was a major component that continued to need development: impulsion.

So I went to learning how to create a flowing, accurate 20-meter circle. Guess what? You need a strong, engaged hind end to keep the horse's balance. In particular, the inside hind leg should reach deeper underneath the body. Without the energy coming from the hind end, the horse will be more likely to be stiff and leaning through the turn.

Then I learned that horses which tend to disengage through a circle will "lose the stifle". So as I went around the circle, I could feel my mare take a misstep in her hind end.

I had always thought that misstep was nothing much to worry about. My mare had a longish back and I knew her stifles were weak. But here I was learning that the misstep was something I could control – if only I learned how to maintain the strength of the hind end through the turns.

All it took was a little bit of forward energy – impulsion.

Forward

It was through these experiences that I was taught the real meaning of the term, "forward". I had always thought of forward as a progression through space. In other words, the horse that was moving "forward" was taking faster steps. There was more wind whistling past my ears and more scenery flew by as my horse reached forward in the gait.

But to my surprise, I realized over time (and through patient explanation and rewording by my instructor) that the horse riding version of forward doesn't really mean forward as defined in a dictionary. The dressage forward is more of a feeling than a movement. So you might have a good rhythm and arc on the circle. You might think that everything is just great. Until you discover what it feels like when your horse really moves with "forward" inclination.

So many things change in the horse when he goes forward! You will be able to feel the difference the moment it happens.

The hind legs stride deeper, and so the strides become longer. You travel over more ground with less steps. It magically feels like the horse becomes more balanced all on his own – less is needed from your inside or outside aids to help him keep from falling in or out. He feels softer in his body. He might give you a more trampoline-y feeling (later I learned that this is called "swing" in the horse's back).

There are also many visible changes that someone can see from the ground. The increased stride length is obvious, and the onlooker might notice an improved "tracking up" – that is, the hind legs step into, or even beyond, the footprints of the front legs. The horse's tail is arched softly to show a round, gently swaying left-right swishing movement. The muscles of the horse's topline, especially behind the saddle, visibly contract and relax in rhythm with the legs.

But the clincher is this: you can feel it and the onlooker can see it.

It's the horse.

For me, it was my horse who told me that *this* is what she had always been waiting for. The first time I found "forward", she sighed and snorted. She released. She softened and started swinging. She balanced. Her rhythm settled.

And she rounded, just a bit.

Round

That was when I knew I was onto something.

At the end of the forward feeling, Annahi did something apparently on her own: she lifted her back, came up in the forehand and arched her neck. Her jaw softened and suddenly we were swinging and floating along, footfalls lightly skipping over the ground – even if only for a few strides! (It took many months and years of practice to be able to maintain this feeling through a variety of movements.)

I had already known all about rounding but it had evaded me in the past. I had worked on getting her to give, to drop her neck, to soften the poll. I had found a way to make her "look" like she was responsive, but never had managed to approach the feeling I had that first time it all came together.

Because of the forward energy (and resulting impulsion), and a well-timed half-halt or two, Annahi rounded. Not because I pulled backward, or tried to put her in position. Not because I let go of the reins and let her move along unaided. No, it was none of those.

She rounded because the increased engagement allowed her to lift her back and soften over the topline. It was almost by accident that I discovered how to truly get a horse to round.

Well, maybe it wasn't exactly accidental. Maybe it was more pre-determined than that. My instructor had been leading me to that point all along. Realistically, if you can get the horse to work from the hind end, you will set up the condition for rounding the back. The natural result of forward is indeed round, assuming that the horse is allowed to move with more expression and allow the energy over the topline.

Forward and Round

This is how the sub-title of this book was born. So many years ago, after finally discovering this most foundational aspect of riding, I adopted this idea of "forward & round" as my mantra.

Because really, if you think about it, forward and round is the root to all riding. It doesn't matter if you are working at the most basic level of riding with a young horse, or if you are working at the highest, most difficult movements: if your horse isn't forward, he isn't round. And the movement is lacking. And the horse is working inefficiently.

It doesn't even matter which discipline you are riding. Every style of riding needs a forward horse – and a forward rider.

Which leads me to my last thought.

The whole concept of "forward" starts with you. And me.

It took some time for me to develop a habit of riding forward. It takes quite a lot of work when you are not used to moving with energy. Even if you get the horse to move with energy, you have to be there yourself. You must try to avoid getting left behind when there is an energy surge.

It takes practice to learn to move *within* the horse's movement.

The Book

This is the second book in the Horse Listening Collection. While the first one, *Horse Listening – The Book: Stepping Forward to Effective Riding* focuses on general topics related to riding, this one is based on training – of both the horse and the rider. The chapters I selected from my *Horse Listening* blog are all related somehow to exercises and ideas which relate to training.

The first section of this book, *The Theory – Forward and Round* is directly focused on everything I have written about the concept of "forward and round". Filled with ideas about how to achieve impulsion and energy, these articles give you some background into the *why* as well as the how of some of the basic exercises and understandings needed to create the type of energy we need.

In Section 2, *The Skill – Rider Development*, we consider many aspects of rider training. From the initial concept of contact, to the use of the seat, rein and leg aids – this section is devoted to rider development and awareness. The end of this section goes deeper into philosophies and practical techniques that can inform better all-around horsemanship.

The third section, *The Training – Getting Deeper Into the Basics*, outlines many exercises that you can use in developing your horse's basic skills. From turning, to bends, neck reins, transitions and suppleness, these ideas are designed to give you some exercises to practice while riding in the ring. All of them are somehow connected to the concept of riding forward and round, whether by increasing energy or inside hind leg engagement.

So, let's get started! It is my hope that you will find many practical tips and ideas throughout this book, as well as a sound explanation of the theory that goes behind the practice.

Kathy

Section 1: The Theory
~ Forward & Round

1 Impulsion: How Two Easy Strides of Energy Might Solve Your Horse Riding Problem

Take Two Deeper Steps Underneath For Better Everything

One of the easiest and most beneficial solutions to many riding problems is to teach the horse to move from the hind end. Why do we harp so much on this topic?

Everything starts with impulsion.
Impulsion starts with the hind end.
Every horse benefits from stepping deeper with the hind legs. If the stride is longer, the hind legs can reach further underneath the body and support the horse's balance with more strength and agility.

The energy derived from the increased impulsion can then travel over the back (topline), allowing for better carriage of the rider and a loftier, bouncier movement, whether in walk, trot or canter. It can help to straighten the horse. It can resolve "behavior" issues. It can even help to reduce tension in the horse's body.

How to Increase Impulsion

For the horse that does not typically, or naturally, use his hind end, taking the two deeper steps might be difficult at first. He might translate the request to mean that he has to move his legs faster, or fall to the inside/outside, or change gait entirely. You might have to learn to coordinate your "go" request with an immediate "no" to help him rebalance rather than to scramble underneath that extra energy.

All it takes is two stronger steps, in the same gait, in the same rhythm, tempo and direction. Use two squeezing leg aids (calf) with a corresponding seat aid for "forward". You may need a half-halt (or two) following the energy surge.

In other words, ask for increased energy but:

- don't let the horse get faster in the gait.
- don't let the horse change gaits.
- don't let the horse scramble because of the extra energy.
- stop him from falling to the forehand.
- help him send the energy straight forward (avoid letting him become crooked).

Teach him to use that burst of energy to lengthen the stride of his hind legs.

You know you are on the right track when:

- the stride becomes bouncier.
- the strides feel longer (you travel over more ground with less steps).

- you feel less overall tension in the horse's body.

Asking a horse for a deeper stride in the hind end results in better impulsion and therefore better weight carriage.

- the horse goes straighter (doesn't fall to the inside or outside on a turn or line).
- you get more "air time".

- the horse begins to round (without you pulling back on the reins).
- the footfalls are lighter when the horse lands.
- for geldings, the sheath sound disappears.
- the horse gives you a heartfelt snort!

The next time you run into tension, leaning, drifting, hollow back, or many other problems that we often think of as resistance or reluctance, try this simple technique. Ask for just two steps of increased energy. Then, evaluate. If you feel there could be more, ask for another two steps.

Increase impulsion in two-step increments, without the expectation of doing more and more and more over the long term.

And see what your horse thinks about it!

2   Five Components of the Ultimate Warm-Up

Every ride starts with a warm-up. But there is a huge difference between a warm-up and a Warm-Up.

It happens all the time.

Horse and rider stroll into the arena, all set to get started on their ride. You can see it from the moment they enter: the rider is walking nonchalantly to the mounting block. Her horse is even less inspired. He ambles along five steps behind her and seemingly requires coaxing, begging – maybe intimidation – to finally set up close enough to the mounting block for the rider to mount.

Once mounted, the "feel" of the ride doesn't improve. The horse continues in his lackadaisical manner. The rider is busy doing everything but riding. She adjusts her clothes, fiddles with the reins, chats with other riders or checks out the car that happens to drive by at that moment. The one thing missing is the enthusiasm and playfulness that characterizes a useful, productive and *enjoyable* beginning to a ride.

****

I have to admit it – the scene above is an exaggeration. But it makes the point: we often get into a warm-up riding rut that becomes uninspiring and tediously routine. Rather than developing an essential first connection with the horse, the opposite happens. Although the rider is right there on top of the horse, there is so little going on between her and your equine partner that they might as well pack it in before they even begin!

Should you ride effectively during a warm-up?

Of course!

Many people think that because the horse starts the ride "cold", that the warm-up has to be slow and under-power. They think that it takes a long time to let the horse's body warm up and therefore, they need to take things easy.

The warm-up proceeds at a fairly leisurely pace. The legs move, the horses truck along and riders feel that in ten or fifteen minutes, the "real" work can start. They do very little during that time – just stay on and get the horse moving.

There may or may not be a canter in that first fifteen minutes or so, but even if there is, the canter is stiff and laborious. After all, the horse shouldn't put too much effort into the movement that early in the ride.

Right?

The Most Important Goal in Horse Riding

Regardless of discipline, what would be the most significant effect a rider would want to have on her horse?

We all want our horses to improve in their athletic development, skill acquisition and connectedness. Much of our rider development and training efforts go into working toward our show or personal goals. These steps and stages are essential to our overall development.

But the best riders aspire to do one essential thing each and every day, regardless of goals and lesson plans: *they work hard to improve their horse's way of going.*

Because proper balance and weight carriage is essential to a horse's longevity. Each and every minute of each and every ride has the potential to contribute to your horse's health and well-being.

Or not.

Why You Don't Want to "Take It Easy" in the Warm Up

Despite your best intentions, the horse that moves incorrectly is the horse that is hurting himself. Without effective use of the hind end, the horse has more difficulty carrying the rider's weight.

The disengaged horse moves with short strides and a hollow back. The body is stiff and difficult to bend and the horse appears to be sluggish. Transitions come slowly. The horse leans into or out of turns. The body shows little suppleness. The topline – the area over the back that carries the rider – sags.

Combined together, it is simple to see why slow and soft is not necessarily the way to go during a warm-up. It just isn't healthy for the horse.

Not that your riding should be harsh or aggressive.

Somehow, you have to find the perfect middle. So what is the alternative?

The Five Components of the Ultimate Warm-Up

Think of the warm-up not as a "warming", but more as a vehicle to get the horse to move well.

The goal of the warm-up is not only to increase circulation and warm up the muscles. It is also to set the horse up to carry the rider's weight with the best balance possible on that day.

Only after the horse is moving well, can the "lesson", or more challenging part of the ride, begin.

Energy

The key to all things riding is energy. However, be sure that the energy doesn't translate into legs just moving quicker.

Instead, use several half-halts to increase the energy without increasing leg speed. Transfer that energy into longer strides, a swinging back and bouncier movement (indicating better use of the muscles).

Topline Use

The horse that uses his topline develops good longitudinal flexion. In clearer terms, being supple over the top of the back means that the horse can carry the rider's weight in a healthier fashion.

The muscles contract and release in tandem to allow the horse's back to act as a muscle "bridge" – thereby relieving some of the pressure off the horse's joints while it moves.

Bend

Every horse has a stiff and hollow side, but letting him go about the ring in tension is not the answer to the problem. In contrast, work on developing a deeper bend left and right early in the ride.

The horse that has lateral suppleness has better balance, hind end use and general comfort.

Straightness

The horse that can bend well is also the horse that can move straight. In order to be straight, the horse's hind footprints should land into the same track as the front footprints.

Beware! True straightness is difficult to develop and takes years of consistent riding to achieve. Most horses travel with some sort of crookedness and imbalance. Repeated exercises will help in achieving enough lateral and longitudinal suppleness to allow for true straight movement.

Rhythm

There is little else in riding that is as essential as rhythm. Every other movement, skill or technique builds upon regular, cadenced footfalls regardless of gait. The warm up should be devoted to developing rhythm – sometimes quicker, sometimes slower and most often, the rhythm that is most ideal for your horse (horses have different *perfect* rhythms).

Your warm-up may take only 15 minutes, or it may use up the majority of your ride on a given day. The length of time devoted to improving your horse's movement is always well spent, regardless of whether it seems to take longer than you initially intended.

Although it seems counter-intuitive to ask for energy and suppleness early in the ride, it makes the most sense when considered from the horse's perspective. Simply put, weight-bearing requires energy, strength and suppleness. Instead of letting your horse move along in an unhealthy fashion, amp up the warm-up, ride effectively, get you and your horse breathing and work toward correct movement right from the get-go.

Then listen to your horse and see what he says.

Here are five practical ideas that you can use to amp up your warm up!

Remember to play everything by ear; some horses need a gradual warm-up, and others need to be more active. Your horse might even need different types of warm-ups depending on the day.

1. Go for a warm-up trail ride.

Heading off for even a casual walk on the trails warms up the horse's mind and body in a way that the ring riding never can. Have a bit of fun for the first 15 to 25 minutes roaming the fields and woods, smelling the fresh air and jazzing up the horse's body.

Move into a trot and maybe even a canter when the time is right, and even start playing with some of the ring exercises right out there on the trails.

Your horse will almost certainly re-enter the riding ring with a better mental attitude. Add energy to enthusiasm and you will find a calmer, softer, more limber horse ready for the following studying session.

2. Go for a canter.

Although it seems counter-intuitive, hopping off into a canter even at the get-go will give your horse more "go-go" right off the bat. You don't have to canter for long; just transition and take a few strides before heading off into a correct, ground-covering trot.

Sometimes, the horse feels tense and tight and a little over-exuberant at the beginning of a ride. A short canter helps let him know he can move when he wants to, and often reassures him in a way that stifling the energy just won't be able to.

Alternately, the sluggish horse benefits from a quick get-yer-blood-going stimulation. Just get into the canter and then evaluate.

You might want to back off into a trot and let him breathe and snort. Or you might get more benefit from a longer canter series of exercises until the horse loosens up and moves more willingly.

3. Use ground poles and get creative.

One way to change the routine while warming up in the ring is to walk/trot/canter through randomly or purposely positioned ground poles. Teach the horse to pay attention to where his feet are going and provide some mental challenge as he learns to negotiate space, striding and timing. Once the horse feels fairly secure, throw in transitions coming into or out of the poles.

Circle away from the pole and return back on a different angle. Go over the poles on a diagonal line. Halt coming to a pole. Canter away from a pole. Decide on a short pattern and take your horse through it several times.

Lunging before riding allows the horse to move without the weight of the rider.

4. Have some cavaletti fun.

Pull out some cavaletti if you have them (or use jump cups to lift jump poles off the ground) and get the horse to elevate his legs. Raise them to the higher height for little mini-jumps or leave them lower so the horse can go over with just a leg-lift.

In both cases, a series of cavaletti can serve as a quick wake-me-up and blood circulating exercise.

5. Play from the ground.

You don't have to ride a horse during the warm-up. Playing with the horse from the ground might be just the exercise your horse wants! Alternate with either a free-lunging session or be more structured with some in-hand work. Although there most certainly is an art to groundwork, and you will notice dramatic development as your skills and ability to communicate improve, there is no harm in some trial and error.

In each of these scenarios, you will notice that your horse warms up mentally and physically toward a more focused, supple and responsive workout. Set up a more productive ride by changing things up, looking forward to new challenges, and stepping out of the round-and-round ring routine that so often becomes our pattern.

Add a little creativity to the beginning of your ride and see what your horse has to say about it!

3   What Being on the Forehand Means to the Horse

We often talk about the ills caused by the horse moving on the forehand, and we dissect and analyze movement in an effort to understand. The idea here isn't to cause guilt and doom and gloom; instead, we should learn all we can and take steps to avoid known problems.

What does being on the forehand really mean, from the horse's perspective? Here are a few thoughts:

1. Lack of balance.

First and foremost, from the moment we get on the horse's back, we are messing around with the horse's balance. Horses that are naturally balanced have to negotiate movement with the weight and (dis-) equilibrium of the rider. Horses that are naturally *un*balanced have to negotiate gravity with not only their own tendencies toward unhealthy movement, but then also with the extra weight of the rider.

2. Heavy on the front feet.

Have you ever heard a horse banging his feet heavily down on the arena footing? If you've ever wondered if that foot pounding might hurt the horse, you'd be right.

3. Pain in the hooves, joints and tendons of the front feet.

Travel long enough on the forehand, and you will create a perfect recipe for eventual lameness. The front legs were not designed to carry most of the horse and rider's weight for extended periods of time.

4. Hollow-backed.

A horse that is heavy on the front end often has to compensate in other parts of his body. So don't be surprised to discover that the horse has to drop his back, or become more "sway-backed." By hollowing out the "bridge" that carries the rider, the horse is counterbalancing the weight that is on the front end. This way, he doesn't actually fall head-first to the ground.

5. Braced neck to counteract gravity.

Similar to having to drop the back, the horse sometimes has to drop the base of his neck and lift his head. This will help him keep going although there is a lot of weight on the front end.

6. Restricted hind-end action and ability.

When the neck is dropped and the back is hollow, the hind end simply cannot support the body. There is no room for the legs to reach forward and under the body, which is where they need to be to receive the bulk of the weight.

7. Short strides.

The strides shorten because the horse becomes more earth-bound. In order to maintain the forehand balance, the horse has to scramble to keep from falling forward. Both the front and hind legs shorten in stride and often speed up in tempo.

8. Trips and stumbles.

Although we like to blame trips and stumbles on external problems such as foot trims, footing and tack, if you watch and analyze carefully, you might notice that the way of going of the horse is often responsible for his regular missteps and occasional falls to the knees.

9. Reins pulling on the mouth.

The rider often feels the imbalance (although might not know who or how it is being caused) and therefore to help correct that awkward feeling, will take up the reins in an effort to hold *himself* up in the saddle.

10. Body-wide tension.

You know the horse that seems forever off but you can't tell exactly what is wrong? It might be caused by the tension in the muscles. A horse that is heavy on the forehand needs to become tense in order to counteract the balance on the front end.

11. Short and shallow breath.

When the horse is tight and tense in the body, he has more trouble breathing. If you can hear deep, strong breaths, and occasional long-winded, body-shaking snorts, then you know you are on your way to allowing the horse to move comfortably underneath you.

12. Mental insecurities.

Unbalanced movement often causes mental strife as well. Horses that have to regularly counteract gravity tend to lose confidence in their riders and sometimes display irritated behaviors such as tail-swishes, pinned ears, bucks and kicks.

If this list makes you cringe, and think that riding on the forehand is the root of all evil, you are beginning to see the point.

There's no two ways about it: being ridden on the forehand causes the horse much difficulty and possibly even physical harm. Always remember that the horse has no choice in the decisions we make as riders.

Therefore, it falls to us – the people who want to enjoy the amazing experience of riding horses – to continually work on our education, improve our skills and regularly challenge ourselves to learn how we can not only NOT cause damage with our riding, but even improve the horse's physical and mental well-being through riding.

4   Frame, Round or Collection?

Which shall it be? Do you know the difference, and in a pinch, would you be able to identify it in a moving horse? Better yet, can you *feel* the difference when you are riding?

We use these words all the time.

We "frame" our horse, we get him to move "round" and we regularly work on "collection". But often, although we're sure we are working on *something*, we don't really know what to call it.

We throw the words around randomly, seeking to describe the feeling we know exists, but not knowing the nuances between the three. To be perfectly honest, most of our horses are rarely, if ever, collected.

These words are not interchangeable.

The three terms are distinct in meaning, appearance and feel. Knowing the difference between them helps you to distinguish between the level of engagement your horse is working at.

The "Frame"

Simply put, a horse is "framed up" when it is travelling in a pre-determined outline. There may be the high frame, which essentially means that the neck is higher than the withers, and there may be the level frame, where the neck is at the height of the withers. In either case, the frame is usually being held in place by rein action (the hands). In comparison to no frame at all, riding in a frame might feel more comfortable and easier on both the rider and the horse.

**This is a frame. Note the hollowed back and
the short hind end stride.**

The dilemma is that regardless of the placement of the head and neck, the back continues to be hollow and the hind end is disengaged. The horse moves on the forehand. The hind legs do not track up to the front footprints, and the front legs stride larger than the hind legs. Often, this body position is held in place by the hands. There is little or no release of the reins and the frame is being protected by a backward pressure that traps the horse's front end and restricts the hind end.

The best giveaway to a frame is that the horse seems to always fall out of the frame – either farther forward on the forehand, or the head and neck arches up and the back hollows even more.

The claim to fame of the frame is that it does not maintain itself without either constant pressure from the hands, or momentary "jerks" on the mouth to communicate to the horse that it should keep its posture in place.

"Round"

A horse travels "round" if there is a certain level of engagement from the hind end. The hind legs reach further forward underneath the body, and the hind stride length approaches the same distance as the front legs. Due to this reach, the hind end dips down slightly while the front end levels out or rises slightly higher than the withers. A round horse is bearing its weight more on the hind end, freeing up the front end to be more expressive and fluid. The rider's weight is carried more evenly with a mildly lifted back.

A release of the reins allows the horse to stride "forward" toward the contact. There is a better sense of freedom in movement than in the framed up horse. To be round, the horse must be "on the bit" or said in another way, "on the AIDS". It is my opinion that most of us can learn to establish round movement most of the time with most horses.

Round - note the deep stepping hind legs, the lightly lifted back and the general forward flow to the movement.

"Collection"

Typically, horses in collection move up and down more than forward, so collection is desired especially in events such as reining, western trail and dressage.

In dressage, collection is the *highest* level of training for the horse. In other words, travelling while collected is difficult and requires a sophisticated level of balance, mental/

emotional control and understanding from the horse. The collected horse has developed the strength to tilt the haunches so the hind legs are far underneath the body, and the front end (head and neck included) are at the highest point. The horse moves in an "uphill" manner.

Collection is achieved primarily by the seat and legs. The hands are the last to act, and ideally, serve to "catch and recycle" the energy produced by the seat and legs. The horse is not kept in place – the collected appearance is the result of the activity of the hind end. Let go of both reins, and the horse should stay in collection for at least several strides.

To be perfectly honest, most of our horses are rarely, if ever, collected. Much of the time, we are working in a degree of roundness – whether more or less round – rather than in collection.

Beginning collection as indicated by the hind end engagement and the elevated front end.

5 How Do You Know Your Horse is Using His Back?

First off, why even bother?

Let's face it: we see many people riding their horses with sunken backs, disengaged hind ends, and heavy footfalls. If *they* do it, why shouldn't we? Are we being conceited, ostentatious, pompous or pretentious? Are we simply just *too picky*?

No, it's none of the above.

It's because we care.

Enough.
To put in the work.

Because it's a fact: learning to feel the back of the horse, especially in movement, is not for the weak-hearted.

It requires hours of dedicated practice, oodles of lesson dollars, numerous requests for forgiveness from the horse, and perhaps most difficult of all, countless adjustments to our internal neural pathways, both physical and mental.

Is all this worth it?

OF COURSE IT IS!

In the long run, our primary motivation for self-improvement in riding is for the sake of the horse's health. We want horses that live well, staying strong and vigorous long into their old age. And a horse that uses his back is carrying the rider's weight to his best advantage.

Feel it.

The round back feels loose, bouncy, rolling, supple. It feels like the horse is having an easy time carrying your weight. He is less on his front legs and more on the haunches.

He gives you the impression that he can stop on a dime or turn on a thought. He is forward, active and content. The energy from the hind end easily flows through the shoulders and you notice larger, longer strides, and bouncier, more active gaits.

If you have trouble with the sitting trot, (you might be shocked to discover that on some horses) you might have even MORE trouble riding the trot of a horse that is moving through his back. This is because the horse's natural gaits become amplified when the back moves freely. You'd be better off posting so that you can encourage your horse to keep his soft, active back.

Here, the horse is using his back. You can see it because of the topline muscles that are active behind the saddle.

The same is true with the canter – the strides become more exaggerated and you feel more swing in the ride. Be prepared to let your lower back flow with the activity – anything less and you'll be stifling the horse's enthusiastic offering.

Basically, if you feel the gaits getting bigger, rounder, and bouncier, then you know you are on the right track!

If you are used to riding a flatter (less engaged) movement, give your body time to learn how to move in tandem with a bigger movement.

The Tight Back:

- feels just that – tight.
- restricts the movement of the legs.
- creates short, choppy strides that lurch and jerk.
- prevents establishment of a good forward-flowing rhythm.
- causes the horse to move on the forehand, taking the brunt of the concussion on the front legs.
- can be the culprit behind sore backs and "mystery" lamenesses.

The irony is that the horse with a braced back can appear to be more "comfortable" to ride, in that the movement is smaller and shorter and thus easier for most riders to follow. If you think your horse feels smooth and comfortable, consider whether or not the smooth feeling is caused by the horse locking his back and preventing movement. Your first clue will be in the size of the stride – if it is a short stride, particularly in the hind legs, then the horse in NOT using his back.

6 Can You Accordion Your Horse?

At our barn, we've turned the noun into a verb. We call it "accordioning" because the horse stretches out over the topline and then, a few strides later, he shortens once again. Much like an accordion, the horse expands and then compresses – over the back. In riding terms, we call it longitudinal flexion.

Starting from an uphill working trot outline, the horse responds to forward-urging aids and a longer rein by lengthening the back muscles. He reaches forward and down into roundness, loosening over the topline and striding deep underneath the body with the hind legs.

Then, a few steps later, the horse transitions back to the uphill outline. The reins shorten while the body shortens and rebalances up and back. The horse resumes the regular working trot.

The Benefits

While the horse is stretching, the muscles loosen to allow for tension to dissipate. Then, when the horse comes back up, the body is more supple, the gait springier. The trick now is to keep the suppleness that was developed through the stretch.

The change of body position and balance encourages the horse to step under with the hind legs, aiding in the development of collection and hind end engagement.

The joints in the hind end "articulate" better – that is, they show more bend and flexion within each stride. This increase in energy translates into increased impulsion, which you might feel through more bounce, more air time, a rounder back, and a lighter front end. It might even encourage the horse to expel a heart-felt snort!

Done repeatedly, the horse learns to loosen at will. Later, the deep stretch may not be necessary. Once the horse has learned to accordion effectively, the results become apparent even with a small stretch and rebalance.

How to Accordion

The first step to an effective accordion is the stretch.

Tightness – in the neck, the base of the neck, in front of the withers, behind the withers and all the way over the back to the croup – blocks the horse's energy. Tension develops and the tightness over the horse's topline becomes visible through a hollowing back, short strides, rushing, dullness or lack of response, and more.

An active stretch with energy going over the topline.

Whether in walk. trot or canter, a well-established stretch over the back is the action that releases the topline. Take contact with the bit, use seat and legs to encourage impulsion, and slowly let the reins out as the horse takes up the slack. The key is that the horse should lower the neck and "chew" the reins from your hands, filling the space given by the reins.

If, at this point, your horses "roots" at the bit – that is, pulls hard in a downward manner, you have two choices.

You can allow it if you think he is having difficulty even understanding the concept. In this case, you should know that rooting is not the end result you want to achieve. At some point, your horse should be encouraged to stretch without pulling. But it can be a place to start if you have difficulty getting any stretch at all.

Or you can continue to hold the rein length – not letting it out – until he softens the pressure and gently reaches to the bit.

Avoid losing complete contact, but continue to allow the rein length so long as the horse keeps reaching for the bit. Take a few strides in this manner.

Cyrus is now in a more uphill outline and balance.

After you have achieved a stretch of several strides (maybe across the diagonal), ask for a little more impulsion with your leg aids and now begin to shorten the reins. At this point, you might need several half-halts to help bring the horse up again, through roundness. Be careful to not just pull on the horse's mouth – this will cause discomfort and tension all over again.

Once the horse has rebalanced to a regular uphill outline, start all over again!

In the end, the horse that can accordion easily and effectively learns to travel with a more supple topline. The process can teach the horse how to release tension in the muscles and become more forward and engaged in movement.

7 Why Most Horses Should Slow Down and How To Do It

Most of us face this problem at some time in our riding careers.

When you put your leg on, your horse only goes faster. Instead of lengthening his stride, or using his back better, he goes faster faster faster. You follow his lead – you post faster just to keep up. Or you ride the increasing canter speed.

It turns into a vicious cycle. He goes faster so you go faster so he goes faster. Sometimes, you might just learn to expect this and think nothing of it.

Other times, you might not be happy with the increasing speed but still not know what to do about it.

If those scenes sound familiar, you might want to slow your horse down. Here's why.

On the Forehand

You probably notice your horse coming more to the forehand. He can't help it – his legs are moving so fast that he HAS to catch himself on the front legs in order to avoid falling. We know that horses (usually) don't literally fall just from a speed increase, but nevertheless, they do have to carry more weight on their front legs to counter the effects of gravity.

Stiffness

Maybe he starts leaning on the bit, getting heavier or stiffer in the jaw. You might notice his movement becoming harsher, with shorter strides that require faster leg movement. Your contact might become heavier and you notice that you have less communication with the horse through the bridle. He cannot bend laterally and there is less and less roundness in his overall outline.

Tripping

Maybe his movement becomes so heavy that he trips here and there. You'd like to blame it on his feet, but you know that your farrier just came out a while ago. You'd like to blame it on a physical problem, but your vet has given you the all-clear.

And still he trips.

If your horse is on his forehand, moving so quickly that he has to scramble to keep his balance, and he moves along in tension, there is a good chance that the odd trip, especially with the front feet, is happening because he simply can't finish the stride in this quick rhythm.

Hollow Back

It is logical that he will hollow his back in order to keep his balance. If the horse is already on the forehand, hollowing the back will allow him to counter gravity. His head will rise, the base of his neck will *drop*, and his bracing back will send tension through the spine.

He will develop a thicker "underline" – rather than sending energy over the topline, he will muscle up the belly area, leaving a flat topline where the saddle sits. Those horses are the ones that always have a "hay belly", regardless of season, corresponding with the unmuscled back (not the same as the obese or wormy horse).

Stress/ Frantic Feeling

Not all horses display this. Some cope quite well, and just truck along with the tension peacefully and with little regard.

But the more sensitive horses cannot be so quiet. They are the ones that communicate the tension: teeth grinding, dry mouths, pinned ears, wild eyes, and some even hold their breath, letting out gasps every now and then. Most of them continue to move along, obedient to the rider. However, the tell-tale signs are there, if you know what to look for.

It's hard to believe that just running fast could cause all these problems in a horse. You can probably imagine it yourself if you're a runner. What would it feel like if you had to run out of your comfortable rhythm, all the time? Can you imagine the tension that would perpetuate in your body if you had to shorten your stride length and move your legs even faster?

What To Do?

Well, the simple answer is to slow down.

The very first thing to do is to not accept the speed. Half-halt the speed and encourage your horse to slow his tempo. He may not even know that he can.

Conversely, when you put your leg on, don't let the horse speed up.

But there is more to it than that. Because if your horse just slows the legs down, he may also let all of his energy "out the back door," thereby reducing his ability to use his body effectively so that he can carry your weight.

Then all you have is slow legs on an equally tense and braced horse!

Now comes the next question: how do you slow the horse's legs down without losing energy?

The Art of Slowing Down Your Horse's Legs Without Losing Energy

Many horses tend to just go faster faster when you ask for more energy. They translate leg aids to speed, thereby coming more to the forehand, heavier on the reins and less balanced. We often talk about how a good rhythm is one of the most basic aspects of good riding. When you find the "right" rhythm for your horse, you might be pleasantly surprised to discover that the balance and weight can improve with little effort on your part.

Your reins lighten up. You stop feeling like you're on a roller coaster going down.

How can you establish a calmer, more reasonable rhythm that will allow your horse to swing more through the back, stride deeper under the body and carry the rider's weight with better strength?

1. Slow Down the Legs

Sounds easy and fairly obvious. First off, just get the horse to stop the leg speed. Do this quickly. In other words, don't let the horse go around the ring a few times before you start to ask him to slow down.

As soon as your horse speeds up, slow him down. Explain to him that your aids do not translate into leg speed. Tell him that he can accept your aids without feeling like he has to brace, go faster, or otherwise become uncomfortable.

Some horses need more convincing than others. Do as much as you need, but as little as possible to get the legs to slow down. This is the first step.

2. Accept Under Power

The next thing that usually happens is that the horse thinks that he has to stop everything. Maybe he breaks to a walk or halt. Maybe he just does this low energy, super strung out under power trot.

But there is more to it than that. Because if you just slow the legs down, you will likely lose a lot of the energy at the same time. Then, the horse moves his legs slowly, yes, but continues to arch his back and drop the base of his neck because in this case, he has to. There is no energy available for him to lift his back to carry the weight of the rider.

So it isn't really only about slowing the legs. The key to finding the horse's ideal rhythm is to slow the legs while maintaining energy.

If, after you slow down the legs, you feel like you and your horse have fallen into quicksand, and each step feels like it has to drag to the next step, you know that's not what you wanted. So after slowing the legs, you need to find a way to continue to encourage impulsion.

3. Gently *Allow* More Energy

If you soften your body and begin to move along with the horse, he will often offer more energy once he settles into the rhythm. You should just ride when he offers an increase in impulsion. Pet him lightly when you feel him take initiative. If the horse doesn't offer, then ask in increments.

When the horse goes to speed his legs, half-halt to slow down gain. Ask for more energy but half-halt the speed. Do this over and over again until the horse finally gives up on the leg speed but starts to engage through the hind end.

Keep in mind that you are part of the equation here too. If you ask for energy but then speed up your posting rate, then the horse will automatically quicken his legs to keep up. Conversely, if you slow the leg speed and then flop in the saddle, becoming dead weight, your horse will also mirror your actions.

So when you ask for energy, make sure you "hover" on the forward phase of the post just a split second longer. Don't fall back to the saddle – carry your own weight down slowly enough to not disrupt the horse's speed.

4. Find the Balance Between Slow But Strong

Sometimes, the horse might slow down and not even know that he can increase his energy. This horse needs gentle encouragement to allow the energy through his body.

Other times, the horse might fluctuate between fast/slow/fast/slow. In this case, it's your job to be the metronome for the horse, and to dictate the slower leg speed after you ask for more energy.

Slow down the horse using your seat and weight aids to resist the speed, but then allow movement immediately afterward to find a better rhythm.

This horse might become confused because he is sure that your leg/seat aids mean faster legs. You have to take the time to change your "language" so that he understands that increased energy does not mean increased leg speed. This horse might need weeks of practice before he is convinced that leg speed is not what you're after.

5. Ride With Commitment

Once you find the energy, you have to ride differently. You can't just push him along and let him brace. So you have to hold your own weight, release a little more through your own back, control your post in the slower rhythm, and basically "be there" with your horse in an energy-but-not-speed feel.

It's Easier Said Than Done!

As with most things in riding, changing your internal speed, increasing your internal energy and putting it all together can be quite the challenge. Because as with all things riding, it starts with you. But it is possible and even if you've never thought about the horse's leg speed, you can do it with some intention.

You know you're on the right track when your horse takes his first few "swinging" steps in slowness.

You know you're getting it when he gives you a snort, and his expression softens or his ears point softly forward.

You can feel it through the saddle, with a sudden trampoline-y feeling that you can describe as a "swing". Maybe your horse arches his neck a bit, lifting the base of his neck and stretching over the top.

And you're definitely there if you find your reins just got longer miraculously on their own, because the horse just rounded and let his energy travel over his topline. (In this case, gently take up the loose rein because you don't want the bit to suddenly loosen in the horse's mouth.)

8 How to Improve the Sewing-Machine Trot

It's called a sewing-machine trot because of the up-and-down movement of the legs. We sometimes call the horse a "leg-mover" and basically mean the same thing.

Essentially, the horse lacks adequate length of stride in the movement.

The legs move but the body does not go anywhere. The horse does not use his torso in the movement. Rather, he is often tight and tense through the body, and there is little swinging in the gait. Sometimes, we mistake the lack of progress as smoothness, but it really is rigidity in horse's the back and joints.

It is easy to get fooled into thinking that the sewing-machine trot is a good trot. When you are on the horse, the frenetic movement might make you think that the horse is working well. He is moving, after all!

But what is sometimes less apparent is that all the movement happens without support from the hind end.

Clues

In fact, the back is often hollow and the energy does not flow back to front. The head may be held high, the base of the neck low, and the majority of the horse's weight falls to the forehand.

One of the easiest identification factors of the sewing-machine trot is lack of "tracking up". The hind leg stride is so short that it falls one or two footprint lengths short of stepping into the front footprints.

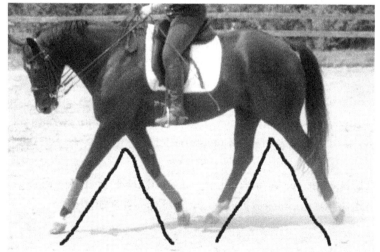

Even stride length indicates a forward-moving horse.

You might also notice that the front legs take a bigger stride than the hind legs. In pictures, the hind legs appear close together underneath the hind end area, rather than drawing equal an upside-down "v" with the one made by the front legs.

What To Do

First, slow the legs down. Reduce the tempo and allow the horse to get better balance. Let his feet catch up to his body, so he doesn't feel like he is constantly running away.

Second, once the tempo becomes more reasonable, address the hind end. Ask for more engagement by using the canter-trot or a similar exercise. Just be careful to not allow the tempo to increase again. Speed is not the intention.

Third, after you feel the burst of engagement, use a half-halt to balance the energy. Don't let it go "out the front end" – rather, contain it and allow the energy to create a longer stride and more movement over the back.

Look for a slower rhythm, but a stronger energy surge. Feel more bounce to the movement. Notice the horse naturally want to round more and reach better for the bit.

Through it all, avoid pulling back. Instead, keep working on half-halts, impulsion and a resulting slow(er) rhythm.

9   On Slobber, Snorts and Sheath Sounds

Everywhere you look, people are missing out on three significant "happy horse" signs. I'm not talking about the perky-eared cute faces looking for treats, or the mutual grooming kind of affection horses share with each other. This time, I'm talking about signs you can see while the horse is being ridden.

It is a fact – horses who move well and freely have a better time during the ride. They learn to look forward to their time in the saddle, and they even improve physically and mentally.

Although we often talk about the hind legs being the "engine" of good movement, it is the back of the horse that is the key to all things great in riding. Think about it – picture the horse with the swinging, supple back and you will almost always recognize the beauty and harmony depicted in the horse's overall way of going. It doesn't matter which discipline or riding style – a good back means good movement and long-term health of the horse.

Read on to find out all about slobber, snorts and sheath sounds, and how they relate to the horse's back.

Thin white "lipstick" indicates a calm and swinging back.

Slobber

Why do some horses have a white "lipstick" while they're being ridden?

Some people say that slobber happens when a horse has his neck so short and the reins are so tight that he can't swallow. They argue that the horse would be able to prevent drooling if only he could open and close his mouth. Maybe his head and neck is positioned in a way that he can't swallow.

Or the problem is in fact the bit that is in his mouth; the piece of metal makes the horse unable to close the lips and swallow. The reasons go on and on.

But surely you have seen a (maybe nervous or tense) horse ridden with a dry mouth for an entire ride. And quite possibly, you've seen a horse lunged with no side reins or any contact whatsoever, carrying his head any which way he pleases, developing a line of foam in the corner of the mouth and around the lips.

And what of the western horse being ridden in a snaffle bit (or any variation of bitless bridles) with very infrequent contact, dripping drool like the highest level dressage horse?

It's All About the Back

I've seen and ridden these horses and experienced their variations of slobber. And I've come to one conclusion: that slobber is connected not so much to the mouth, jaw or swallowing – but to the back of the horse. Develop movement from the hind end, get a nice rhythm and back swing, and presto: discover the path to slobber.

If you think about it, the root to all good in riding rests in the back. If you can encourage an elastic, round, swinging back, you know your horse is on his way to riding pleasure. Not only does he benefit from the work; chances are, he might actually be enjoying it.

However, don't stop there. It's not only the horse's back you have to consider – think about *your* back too. Because your back can be holding your horse's back back (did you follow that?), which results in tension all around.

If your back is resistant or unmoving, the same will happen to your horse. He won't be able to carry your weight effectively, nor will he be able to let the energy flow through his topline.

So freeing your back up and developing more mobility will also lead you to slobber from your horse's mouth.

Snorts

Happy horse sign number two is the snort.

Physically, the snorts happen when the horse takes a deeper breath. He might reach farther underneath the body, work more through the abs or put in a sudden moment of effort. For whatever reason, he then has to take a deeper breath and then he lets it all out in a body-shaking snort. Sometimes, the snort is accompanied by a neck arching or reaching forward that might catch you off guard if you're not expecting it.

In any case, the snort is a releasing/relaxing/letting go of tension and yes, you might notice the horse's eye soften or his gait become more buoyant. Watch a little longer and you might see him settle in his work, find his rhythm or soften in the jaw. You might also see some accompanying slobber!

Sheath Sounds

Now this one is the clincher. Of course, if you ride a mare, you miss out on the most obvious, tell-tale sign of a tight back. In geldings, the tight back causes a tight sheath area, which then results in air movement – that sound you hear EVERY stride the horse takes.

People often say that the sound is caused by a dirty sheath area. But if you own or care for a gelding regularly, chances are that you can honestly say that the sheath has been cleaned and yet the sound continues. So what gives?

Yes, folks, it's all about the back yet again.

Try this: when you hear the sound, go for a 3-5 stride canter from the trot. Then trot again. Make sure you half-halt the trot as you come out of the canter, so that the horse doesn't just trot faster faster faster. Rather, you want to use the canter to add more impulsion to the trot. Feel for more bounce, more air time between strides and/or a rounder back. See if you can get a snort.

And then listen for the sheath sound. Maybe it stops for a few strides. Maybe it isn't quite as loud. Or maybe it goes away altogether. If you "listen" carefully enough, you will begin to recognize a pattern to the sound.

Maybe you can make it go away for only a couple of strides. Pay attention to what caused the sound to go away. Then try to duplicate it. Maybe your horse is too tense for the sound to ever go away. But give it a good try, every ride. Eventually, you might be able to make it go away just using your riding skills. And you'll know that your horse is using his back in a healthier manner.

So there you have it: three sure-fire ways of knowing if your horse is actually loose in his back!

Section 2: The Skill
~ Rider Development

10   Riding For the Rest of Us

We watch in awe as the Super Horses break records, thrilling and inspiring us in our respective disciplines. Without doubt, specialized breeding programs have developed bloodlines to seemingly new heights in the various equestrian sports.

At the top levels, horses are more suited to their events: they jump higher, piaffe with more suppleness, run faster and longer, slide further than ever before. Their conformation is nearing "perfection" more than ever in the history of horse breeding.

While we marvel at the exceptional performances of these elite horses and their riders, most of us come home to our "ordinary" and perhaps even less than perfect horses. Many of us own just one horse over a number of years and recognize that we have chosen that particular horse perhaps not for his exceptional physical characteristics, but rather for other qualities such as temperament, rideability or even something as intangible as emotional connection.

It is possible that your horse is too small, or too large. Maybe your horse is built naturally downhill or with a long, weak back.

Other common faults could include the horse with the club foot, the winging or paddling front legs, or the horse with the undeveloped hind end.

Yet all these horses have one thing in common – they can be lifelong partners assuming we can become effective and educated riders, always working towards self-improvement and that of our horse.

So, if we are not going to (be able to?) ride that perfect horse, what can we do to enjoy our favourite four-legged friend for years to come?

1. Know your horse's conformation faults.

Study the details involved in how your horse is built, and work with a good instructor on overcoming those physical characteristics that might impede his soundness and progress in the long run.

Learn how to get him to work from the hind end, develop his longitudinal and lateral flexibility, and help him become a happier horse through deliberate and kind exercises that enhance his suppleness and strength.

2. Know your own physical weaknesses.

Seek help in discovering your own idiosyncrasies. Do you have a tendency to lean one way? Are you too constricted in one part of your body and too loose in the other?

Any imbalances on your part will affect your horse in the long run – so find out what you need to work on and take steps to develop strength and flexibility where you need it the most, OFF the horse's back! Then, do your best to transfer the skills while riding.

3. Don't ignore your strengths.

What are you good at? What can your horse do easily? Use that movement as your "play" time – after a tougher series of movements, or as a celebratory "game" for a change of pace.

Whether you want to work on your difficulties or your horse's, don't avoid the tough stuff! Get out there and give it a try – just cut yourself some slack and know that you might not ride like the elite athletes, and your horse may NEVER match the top equines. However, you can both definitely improve and develop a little at a time.

You just might be surprised at what you *can* achieve!

11   A Cautionary Horse Tale

Once you decide to ride horses, you put into place a domino effect of consequences, which will occur whether you are conscious of them or not. It is like a rule of nature – the results are the results regardless of your intentions, desires and motivations.

And so you proceed to put your weight on the horse's back, asking him to move in tandem with your (sometimes uncoordinated) instructions, changing the weight distribution on his back and legs and (quite) possibly upsetting his balance. Most horses will proceed to do their best to support you even to their own physical detriment.

This is where brain must meet brawn. At the intersection of movement and time, you find yourself in a constant state of disequilibrium and re-balancing. And the question begs to be asked: what can you do to not only avoid being the source of damage to the horse, but instead develop enough skill to become the active agent that develops, rehabilitates, and even improves the horse from its natural state?

Learning how to ride so that you are not a burden to the horse takes time, knowledge, perseverance, self-discipline, at least a minimal amount of athleticism and yes, even sweat and tears.

Making the commitment to stick through the learning curves (so many plateaus and even some steps backward before going forward again) seems to at times test you to the depths of your character – to the point that you think, "Was this my idea of *fun*?!"

But don't despair – this is not a tale of doom and gloom. It is a hopeful tale, one that inspires rather than frustrates. For there are so many glorious experiences just waiting around the corner, if only you just stick to your daily work, and put in the (sometimes huge) effort into improving your skills. You will know when those moments occur, because *those* are the moments that keep you working so hard for more.

Regardless of where you are in your development as a rider, in the back of your mind you must always be seeking for the better way. This is the path that promotes confidence in yourself as the rider, and for the benefit of the horse.

This is the way that improves you to the point that you and your horse become of one mind and body, and most importantly, it allows your horse to develop positively mentally and physically, making him a happier, better adjusted, more settled, sounder horse for many years of partnership ahead.

And when that happens, relish the moment, and keep searching for more of the same!

12   Fourteen Ways to Communicate While Riding Your Horse

How do you communicate with your teammate when you ride?

Athletes from other team sports learn to communicate with each other as an essential part of their activity. Hockey, soccer, basketball, cricket – or any other game where players rely on each other – requires excellent communication between players.

Regardless of the rules and the playing field (or rink), athletes coordinate with each other through voice, signals and body language. In fact, you could say that aside from raw talent, communication might be the single most important factor in a team's success.

Horseback riding is unique among team sports precisely because of the horse that becomes your athletic partner. The difference between other sports and ours is that we must learn to communicate to our teammate in less obvious ways.

We need to learn a language that relies on physical movement and feel – something very alien to human beings who don't have to interact with a 1200 pound partner.

Want to improve communication with your horse? Use these "natural" aids in rhythm with the horse's movement, at the right moment within the stride, and see how you can speak in full sentences through the body.

Seat

The seat is where all riding starts. Without a stable, balanced seat, you will always have trouble staying with your horse. But more than that, you can communicate so many things through your seat, that your hands and reins can eventually become the icing rather than the cake.

Calves

Soft, "breathing" calves can communicate confidence and reassurance to the horse. Use a stronger calf aid to ask for bend or reinforce a two-track movement but then release again to reward and reinforce your horse's response.

Lower Back

Although the lower back is technically part of the seat, it can send distinct messages through the seat that are not necessarily connected to the buttocks. Brace with the lower back to resist the horse's forward movement, or release and follow to amplify it.

Knees

The knees deserve to have their own section here because they have a subtle but definite effect on the horse's movement. Often, riders release their seat only to pinch with their knees. The resulting conflicting messages could cause the horse to hollow his back or slow down despite the seat aids. Release the knees moments at a time and see how your horse responds. If he gives you rounder, bolder movement, you know that you have been gripping too tightly with the knees.

Keep them soft (but not so soft that you lose balance) and see what your horse thinks.

Thighs

The thighs have a similar action. You can grip through the thighs to resist and restrict movement or you can soften, which will allow your seat to move along with the horse. The thighs also help the rider in finding a deeper balance in the saddle by settling into the saddle.

Finally, they can reinforce your bending aids so that there is contact with your horse's side from the seat, through the thigh, to the calf and foot. This is the imaginary "wall" we speak of when we want to create an aid that the horse will step away from to create the bend or lateral movements.

Shoulders

Your shoulders hold more power that you can imagine! Keeping a vertical line between your shoulders, hips and heels will enable you to move in balance with your horse.

The shoulders can also help in the maintenance of the horse's balance. If you lean back within the movement (i.e. don't stay leaning back), you can influence your horse to shift his weight further to the hind end without jerking the bit in the horse's mouth or causing him to hollow his back.

Head

The average human head weighs 10 pounds! Use your head purposely and it can also act as an aid, and influence your other aids. In general, keep your head up and eyes looking slightly ahead of your horse.

If you want a bend, turn your head slightly toward the bend – but don't overturn your head or it will encourage an overbend in your body as well as your horse's!

Buttocks

Yes, these can also "talk" either in conjunction or not with the seat. Squeeze the gluteus maximus and lighten the load on your horse's back. Soften the glutes and become heavier in order to deepen your seat aid or reinforce your rhythm.

Feet

The feet factor into communication as well. Keep your feet parallel to the horse's side to follow and "breathe" along with the calves. Turn the toes out to create more of a wall especially for a lateral movement. Alternately, take the foot off to invite the horse's rib cage into that space.

Fingers

We always teach that the fingers should be closed in a soft, light fist so that the communication going to the mouth is consistent and steady. Sponging the reins can wiggle the bit in the horse's mouth and conversely, closing the fist can keep the horse from pulling the reins out of your grasp. Some moments might require a more solid feel while other moments can be "butterfly" soft. But in all cases, avoid opening and closing the fingers.

Elbows

We've spoken about the effect of the elbows before. In general, the effect of the elbows can be similar to the fingers.

Keep a soft bend so that you can follow the horse's movement. Momentarily hold them on your sides to resist for a half-halt.

Eyes

The eyes deserve their own section here because they can control so many aspects of your body. If you can find your peripheral vision, you can communicate softness through your skull and shoulders, which then can influence the rest of your torso and aids.

Use your eyes to pinpoint a spot in the ring when you want to abruptly influence the horse (say, during a sideways deek when you were asking for a turn) but return to your peripheral vision to resume going with the horse.

Breath

Many people write about the breath as it relates to horse riding. It is essential to breathe uniformly while you move with the horse. If you find that you hold your breath at times, break the pattern by singing (even under breath – no one needs to hear!). Find a fun song that you know well and sing in rhythm with your horse's movement. You'll find that your body releases without any forcing on your part.

Voice

You probably know from experience that voice can be a huge support to your body aids. If you can teach your horse certain words or sounds, you can give him a heads-up while you apply your body aids or even before. Just remember to keep it quiet if you enter the dressage ring!

*****

Of course, as we all know, there is no such thing as riding with aids separated from each other. Although you can learn to develop arms and legs independent of the seat, and we can dissect each body part to the core, the secret to riding is that *everything you do* is received by the horse in one moment.

Riding is about using all the aids in coordination.

So riding is more of a holistic exercise that involves the whole body, than moving a hand or a leg or sitting in a given position.

But by breaking down the aids, we can isolate the ones we need to develop. Then we can go back to putting it all together again – when we are on the horse's back!

13 The Dynamic Dependency of Horseback Riding

First scenario: You go to the clinic and watch it work perfectly for the horse and rider. You come home and try the new technique and after a short time of pseudo-success, it all falls apart (again)!

Alternate scenario: Your coach teaches you something new, and the lesson goes well. Then you ride on your own and simply cannot get the same results. At first, you might blame the horse. Or you might think that the clinician/coach did not explain it well enough. Maybe it is the weather, the saddle, the bridle… you get my drift!

You wonder – why does it work for others when it doesn't work for you?

The dynamic dependency of riding

There is no getting around it: there is an interconnectedness in riding that you simply cannot escape. Everything has to "jive" before the final picture of ease and comfort presents itself. In fact, horseback riding can essentially represent the highest sense of "holistic" that you can ever imagine.

In riding, nothing can be done in isolation. If you change even your weight from one side to another, or from forward to back, you can instantly feel the difference it makes to the horse. If you learn that new skill at the clinic, and you bring that home, beware that one single change will not be effective if the rest of what you are doing stays stagnant.

What I'm trying to say is this: if you think one skill/technique/method/movement will be the answer to your riding dreams, you have to know that you will be disappointed.

Everything depends on everything else.

Your horse will quickly explain to you that there is more than one aspect to ANYTHING in riding. There is no miracle bit, no fantastic rein aid, no leg position, or anything else in isolation that will make the difference you are seeking.

The secret to riding is that *everything matters*. If you want that new leg position to be effective, you probably need to shift your weight, move your shoulder, flow better through the seat, half-halt more accurately, even *think calmly* (and so many other aspects) that it might become discouraging to think of all the parts to the whole.

But there is hope! It comes with patience, perseverance, hard work and a sense of humour. You need to know that there is no "all-or-nothing" solution to your riding woes, and you must seek *all* the answers over time.

You might find that the super-duper rein aid will in fact be beneficial if you combine it with a small change in your position and a better flowing seat. Of course, you need a good eye on the ground to help you along your path, and you need to expand your awareness of the many skills that are required to produce the final product.

****

Back to the rider in the clinic who demonstrated the technique so well: she probably made all the minute changes to her position/aids to make the miracle aid work effectively.

In your riding lesson, chances are that your instructor can catch all the small corrections that need to be done during your ride. Although everything falls together while she is teaching you, you will likely only remember parts and pieces that will not be as effective when used in isolation.

Once you have the experience and feel to make small adjustments, the area you are focusing on will indeed become significant to the overall picture.

Over time, you will learn to rub your belly, pat your head and chew gum at the same time! Don't be resentful of the practice required to develop all the fine details in riding. In fact, celebrate each time you are facing frustration, because this is the *real* stuff of riding.

And your horse will thank you for it!

14   Demystifying "Contact"

Sometimes it feels like the word "contact" has other-wordly connotations. Is it related to celestial retrogrades, or long-told mythical verbal traditions, or is it a yogic position unreachable by the average equine enthusiast?

Simply put, it is a must learn skill that every horseback rider needs in their toolbox. In fact, contact as it relates to horse riding is a lot less mystifying than it might initially appear.

It is true that the *perfect* contact is almost unattainable, and you can devote a lifetime to developing the ultimate level of contact between you and your horse. But to think that correct and effective contact is something out of the reach of the average rider is simply not true.

Developing contact with your horse is very much like shaking hands with a person.

Picture This

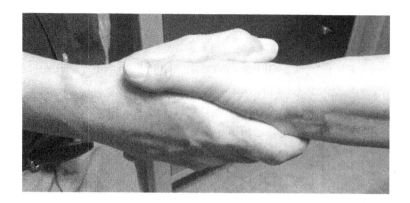

You reach for the person's hand and the other person reaches for yours. You close fingers relatively gently (we are not considering those strong shake-your-shoulder-off aggressive shakes!) around each other's hand and you mutually lift and drop your hands in the shake.

In general, it feels nice to shake someone's hand. You both show a willingness to meet in the middle and share a physical bond that connects you together.

Here's another picture: We've all seen partners in figure skating reach for each other's grasp as if by some mutually-shared secret that is known only to them. As they skate along, their "contact" changes from hand to hand, forward to backward, always meeting at a designated point, never appearing forced or contrived. We see the results – almost imperceptible communication that enables both partners to use each other's talents to bring out the best in each other. You could imagine a similar situation in ballroom dancing and other such activities.

And so it should be with a horse.

To initiate contact, you *must* shorten the reins. Don't let anyone tell you that it is "cruel" to shorten the reins on a horse. In fact, it could be more damaging to drop the contact on your bit by letting your reins droop. The drop of the reins will cause the bit to move in the horse's mouth. At the very least, by virtue of the lifting and dropping motion from the horse's own movement, a long rein can cause discomfort on the horse's tongue and bars of the mouth.

So… **shorten the reins *but don't pull*!**

The trouble that many riders get into with contact is that they think that short reins means pulling reins. This is far from the truth. Once you have achieved a useful rein length that allows you to hold the bit in the horse's mouth, your next job is to keep that contact steady.

This is where it gets tricky – take up contact, and then keep it there (prerequisite: strong core muscles and hands that are independent of the seat so they can respond to the horse's needs rather than using the mouth for balance).

Next, invite the horse to *reach forward into the contact*.

This is the part of the "handshake" where the horse goes to meet you. The trick here is that you have to create room within the contact for the horse to literally reach slightly forward with the whole body (including but not limited to the head and neck) to *meet your hands at the end of the bit*.

Initiate the horse's reach by asking for more impulsion – from your legs and seat – and then allowing the energy over the horse's back and into your hands. Create a millimeter of space (*don't drop the reins!!*) for your horse to reach into. If you feel your horse surge forward into a rounder body outline (creating a "lifted back" to carry you with), you know you're on the right track!

What do you do when you have contact?

Maintain it and then try something new!

Work toward getting your horse "on the bit". You might want to ask the horse to reach further underneath itself for more collection. You might want the horse to transition into another gait. Maybe you want a bend, or a counter bend. In any case, you will always be working toward promoting a better weight bearing position for your horse while you are on his back.

The point is that without contact, you will always surprise your horse into the new movement, you will likely cause discomfort or even pain in the horse's mouth, and there will often be inconsistencies in your communication.

One thing to remember is that the quality of your contact can always be improved. We do always seek "better" contact, developing in the softness, lightness, gentleness and effectiveness of the touch. Each new circumstance requires a small adjustment to the quality and level of the contact, and each horse has different requirements and tolerances.

However, one thing remains true: a horse in good contact is a happy horse! And isn't that what we are all aiming for?

Note: Different disciplines require different "styles" of contact (i.e. western riding using curb bits) but there is nevertheless always a minimum level of contact that enables the horse to work at its optimum.

15   On Bubbleneck and Marshmallow Contact

As you probably already know, just when you think you know something, you realize that there is so much more left to be learned. Recently, this epiphany happened to me (yet again) and this time, it was about developing a better contact.

Somehow, just when I finally felt that my contact was becoming soft and supple and kind, I discovered yet another deeper level of contact that blew away what I thought I knew. Of course, it was just a momentary tease.

When these new, exhilarating feels saunter into your world, they rarely stay around long enough for you to be able to really get a good sense of what just happened. You're lucky if you can even just recognize (and maybe memorize) the feel before it flits along on its way.

And so it was that while I thought I was teaching Roya something, she ended up teaching me something right back. Please bear with me as I use these "fluffy" words to try to describe feels and visuals.

Bubbleneck

Next time you have a chance, watch some horses as they're ridden in the ring. Look at their necks as they go around. Are they "filled up" – topline muscles supple and bouncy in the rhythm of the movement? Or are they flat and almost cardboard-like, not responsive to the movement, braced and stiff and still?

Bubbleneck is a term I came up with to describe what the neck looks like when energy is flowing over the topline as the horse moves. The muscles at the top of the neck bulge and ripple under the skin, working in tandem with the rhythm of the legs.

In contrast, the braced neck shows the exact opposite – the top of the neck is thin and unmovable (and the horse likely moves stiffly left and right) and the "underneck" bulges. Over time, the muscles under the neck might overdevelop. Or, your horse might be naturally predisposed to developing an underneck, due to conformational reasons.

The key to developing a nice bubbleneck is to get the horse to lift the base of his neck. This lift allows the horse to move more freely through the shoulders and remain in better balance in the front end. Although the feel is initiated from the hind end, it's what you do with the energy in the front end that either drops the base of the neck or lifts it.

Bubbleneck occurs because of a strong, active topline and a released underline.

Now, some horses might have incredibly good conformation and front-end strength. They can almost always move with a bubbleneck no matter what you're doing. But many others, and especially those with a downhill conformation, will have more of a tendency to just brace, drop the base of the neck and move along on their forehand.

In this case, what you do affects the horse either positively or negatively, depending on the result of your aids.

Marshmallow Contact

So while I was working on getting my horse to lift the base of her neck while moving in a steady, rhythmical and energetic trot, she suddenly took the bit and softened in every aspect. My fairly steady, fairly light contact morphed into something that I can only describe as "marshmallow."

It was soft, fluffy, malleable and yet springy like a marshmallow. It was also as crushable – so if my (always closed!) fist tightened just past the "too strong" threshold, the contact would squeeze away just like a marshmallow would collapse into itself with too much strength. And so Roya and I floated along during those precious few strides, with this marshmallow-y feeling, in balance and somehow NOT on the hands but seamlessly moving together in tandem, with much less emphasis on the hands for direction.

And then it all fell apart!

Of course, now I'm looking for both bubbleneck and marshmallow contact in all my riding, through all the movements including walk and transitions. I can find that feel much of the time, if not all of the time. But as I get better at asking for bubbleneck and allowing for marshmallow contact, Roya is having an easier time allowing it to happen.

How To Bubbleneck

Bubbleneck must come first. Because without the lifted base of the neck, the horse's balance is already affected negatively.

Then "contact" can never get past a push/pull level. Here's a breakdown of what I think I'm doing.

Initiate Impulsion

Squeeze with the lower legs, encouraging a higher level of impulsion and energy, and a lifting of the horse's back.

Not a bubbleneck!

Follow With the Seat

Immediately allow the energy "through" with your seat. Encourage the horse's initiative to move forward. You might need to allow more movement than you're used to in your core and lower back to allow the horse to swing through his back.

Half-Halt

I know it always comes back to the half-halt! But you must half-halt at the end of the energy surge, or the horse will simply have too much energy and fall to the forehand.

Too little (or no) half-halt will just send the energy forward and down, putting the horse even more on the forehand and necessitating more bracing through the front end.

Too much half-halt will stunt the energy and not allow it to "go through" enough, thereby stopping the hind legs from stepping under. So you have to fiddle long enough to find the just right amount of half-halt (all horses are different).

Find the Bubbleneck

Now you have to pay close attention to your feeling receptors. You can also probably see the topline muscles of the neck as they start to "bubble" (or not).

Figure out what it takes for the bubbleneck to appear, and why it goes away.

Contact!

As you can establish a longer bubbleneck, you should be able to feel the change in the level of your contact. Finding marshmallow contact isn't about taking more or less pressure on the reins. It's more about creating and maintaining an ideal balance. Make sure you keep a steady contact and wait for the horse's change of balance to allow for the better contact.

16 One Simple Way to Quiet Your Hands While Riding Horses

Well, by now, you might already know that when something is "simple" in horse riding, it isn't necessarily easy! Quieting your hands falls into this category.

What is this simple way? Well, stop using your hands!

It's pretty simple to not use your hands, but it might not be so easy to increase the use of your other aids in lieu of the hands. If you're anything like me, and you developed the habit of controlling pretty much everything from the horse's mouth long ago, then you know how difficult it can be to reduce your reliance on your hands.

However, I'm here to tell you that it can be done. It *is* possible to go to your other aids and save your hands for only two things: the end of the half-halt (in order to help with rebalancing the horse) and straightness/flexion.

The hands do play a role in the half-halt. I've explained it in detail along with the other aids here and more of a basic description here. They also can maintain the horse's straightness, particularly in the shoulders, especially when you are on a bend or turn. They also can help with maintaining the flexion of the jaw (usually in the direction you are going).

Other than that...
... the hands should and can sing poetry in the horse's mouth and help him develop confidence and strength within his own movement.

The rest of the body can take over much of the in-movement communication with the horse. And this is where the difficulty comes in for some of us. It takes a quite a lot more coordination and core strength to aid your horse through your seat, legs and body. But with practice and guidance, it can be done.

Only then can your horse lighten on his feet and carry you with more comfort and strength. And for the rider, there is a sense of freedom that comes along with the reduced reliance on the hands.

4 Aids to Use in Lieu of the Hands

The Seat

The rider's seat is the root of all good in horseback riding. Not only does the seat keep your balance and allow you to

85

move in harmony with your horse, but it also sends an almost unlimited amount of communication to your horse.

Because, you see, the seat is the largest area of contact with your horse, and it sits (pun!) literally in the middle of the horse. From there, you have the opportunity to send almost invisible signals to your horse. And he will likely respond easily just by virtue of the fact that it is easier for him to move from the middle of his body than the front.

The Weight

The use of weight is an off-shoot of the use of the seat and they work together in tandem. You could ride with a balanced seat that isn't indicating anything in terms of weight, or you can use your weight to your advantage. Let's imagine a turn – if you can weigh your inside seat bone into the turn, you will invariably help your horse turn easier and with better balance. How about a leg yield? Use your weight aid to invite your horse into the direction of the movement.

The Legs

The legs are critical for clear communication. The inside leg works on bend and keeping the inside shoulder moving straight. The outside leg is responsible for asking the hind end to stay in line with the front end (and not swing out, for example). It also is the main initiator of bends, shoulder-ins/haunches ins, canter departures and turns.

You can also "step into the stirrups" to support your seat aids, or to create a stronger leg if the horse is moving into it. The more educated you and your horse get, the more meaning you can offer through your leg aids.

The Voice

Especially at the beginning, either for a novice rider or horse, the voice can be a welcome reinforcement of the body aids. If the horse is young or relatively untrained, voice cues might not initially carry much meaning, but they can serve to calm the horse or conversely, add a little "spice" into the horse's movement (if you need increased energy).

Voice cues can be words or sounds, depending on how you want to develop them. You do not have to be loud to be effective. Use consistent voice cues and your horse will in fact be able to understand and predict what you want.

Well, there you have it! Riding with less emphasis on the hands is possible and highly recommended, not only for your pleasure, but for your horse's comfort as well. Although it might take more time than you might initially want to invest, developing your other aids to the point of clarity is well worth the effort.

17   Twenty Signs That Your Horse Benefits From Your Riding

Do you sometimes wonder if what you are doing with the horse is beneficial to him? Are you occasionally unsure of how well your riding/training program is going?

One of the surest ways to know if you are being helpful to through your riding is to listen to the horse. If you know how to interpret his signs and communications, all your questions will essentially be answered, especially in terms of the impact of the ride on your horse.

Are you following your horse's movement?

Are you asking for/allowing enough impulsion?

Do you "commit" your body to the forward motion you're asking for?

Is the horse learning to/allowed to stretch over the topline so he can more effectively use his musculature to carry you?

These questions (and more) can be answered by correctly reading the horse's responses to your requests. Although many of these signs can be seen from the ground or during groundwork, the advantage of these horsey "yes answers" is that they can be identified *while you ride*. Here are some ways to know if you are on the right track:

- the horse gives an emphatic snort.
- the horse licks and chews through the movement.
- the horse is calmer at the end of the ride than he was at the beginning.
- the horse's topline looks fuller, even just moments after the ride.
- the horse's stride becomes longer, bouncier and more cadenced.
- the horse bends deeper with less rein aid.
- movements come easier after a few repetitions.
- the horse reaches higher/wider/longer with the hind end.
- the eyes get soft.
- the horse's expression is calm.
- the horse's ears fall (of sometimes flop) gently to the side unless he is "listening" to your aids, at which point the ear will momentarily come back to you.
- the horse softens his poll/jaw upon contact.
- transitions come easily.
- bends and turns are softly negotiated.
- he can stay straighter in his body while moving on or off the rail.

- the horse engages his hind end quickly and easily without tensing or bracing through the additional energy.
- the back becomes softer, especially in the trot.
- the tail lifts slightly during movement.
- the hind legs track up or over-track.
- the horse's overall body outline rounds rather than hollows.

18   What Do Leg Aids Mean?

The leg aids are one of the most basic, "natural" aids we have to communicate with the horse. All riders regularly use their legs to give messages to the horse, but much of the time, the legs mean go faster or change gait.

Fortunately, there are many other uses for leg aids. Using them for the "go" message is good to use when you are a novice rider and beginning to grapple with the various aids. However, as you develop your skills, your aids can evolve to become less intrusive and more specific.

Instead of relying on them only to get the horse to move his legs faster or transition to a new gait, we might discover more involved messages that can be given with a sophisticated leg aid.

Although there are many variations of how to use your legs, we will discuss their *purpose* in this article. Also, the other aids (weight, hands, seat bones) must be employed along with the legs for all movements, but here we will look only at the legs.

What the leg aids do not mean:

Gait change.

Riders are taught early in their education that the legs should be positioned in particular ways to indicate gait change. While this is an effective method to communicate a particular gait to a horse, riders often confuse the two leg kick as a gait change. Soon enough, the horse thinks, "upward transition" to any leg use.

It might seem that a quick change of gaits is desirable. However, what you miss out on by letting the horse "leak" into the next gait is the opportunity to allow the horse to use his back and engage within a gait.

To get a fluid gait change, use your leg positions but initiate the movement with your seat.

Tempo change.

Changing leg speed is somewhat related to the gait change above. If the horse can't change gaits in response to leg, then surely it must go faster within the gait! The problem is that by allowing the horse to go faster faster faster, you suddenly find yourself on the forehand and out of balance. Half-halts become difficult to do and you often have to resort to pulling the horse to slow down and regain balance.

Once again, regulate the tempo with your seat.

Pain.

People often feel that it is necessary to use strong kicking legs. Kicking is unfair if it is being used to inflict pain. Just as with any other aid, legs (and spurs) should be used as a method of communication and not for causing discomfort or distress to the horse.

What they do mean:

Go (impulsion)!

Leg aids tell the horse to step deeper underneath the body with the hind legs. There might or might not be a gait change involved. However, the leg speed should not change nor should the gait change be initiated solely by the legs. The legs aids may result in a slight whiplash effect for the rider as the horse engages the hind end and creates a stronger, more active stride. This is good!

Reach for the bit (longitudinal flexion).

Two legs can encourage a horse to lift his back. Along with impulsion, the horse can learn to allow the energy over the topline so that the back will lift, round and therefore the horse can reach forward to the bit.

Bend (lateral flexion).

Stepping away from the leg aid allows the horse to bend "through" the rib cage. The space that is created by a sideways shift of the ribs allows the horse to bring the inside hind leg deeper under the body. This is often helpful for the horse to balance better through turns and corners. These leg aids are also useful for shoulder-in and haunches-in.

Step away (lateral movement).

The leg aid that lingers is asking the horse to step away in a lateral manner. These leg aids are used for movements such as leg yields, half-pass and full pass (a.k.a. side pass).
Bear in mind that the legs are just a part of the overall communication process that goes into aiding the horse. If we are clear on why we use leg aids, the "how" becomes easier and makes more sense.

19 Stop Kicking the Horse!

Too often, riders are determined to make their horses go with a swift kick or two (or three). At best, the horse lurches forward with arched back and raised neck, scrambling to get his legs underneath him despite being thrown to the forehand. At worst, the horse becomes resentful of the leg aid and learns to resist or even demonstrate his discomfort by kicking out, rearing or bucking.

Did you know that leg aids are used for more than just "go"? Leg aids are such an integral part of your ride that you simply can't do without them!

As you become a better rider, you will discover that the legs have so many messages to communicate other than "go".

Talk to different riders and they'll tell you the various uses of leg aids. Here are a few examples:

1. Impulsion

The most important result coming from your leg aids is impulsion. Ideally, the lightest calf squeeze should communicate an increase in movement from your horse. Two legs squeezing at the same time ask for a "scoot forward", causing the horse to tuck his hind under and release a surge of energy forward.

Physiologically, the horse's hind legs should step deeper underneath the body and allow the horse to begin the process of carrying more weight in the hind end.

2. Stride Length

Ideally, a deeper reach should mean a rounder back and an increase in stride length. Paired with half-halts, the energy obtained can be redirected in many ways – to a longitudinal stretch over the back, to a higher head and neck elevation or to more animated action through the entire body.

One leg can be used to create a deeper hind leg stride on that side of the horse. Theoretically, you could influence just one hind leg with the corresponding leg aid.

3. Bend

Use of one leg aid should encourage your horse to move away from that pressure. True bend (i.e. not a neck bend) should always begin at the seat, be reinforced by the leg, and then be contained with the reins.

4. Hind end position

Using your leg behind the girth should indicate that the hind end steps away from that pressure. Use of your outside leg behind the girth encourages the horse to work into a haunches in ("travers") position. Using your inside leg behind the girth is the key to the renvers, when the horse bends to the outside of the direction of movement.

5. Keep Moving

Two legs used at the same time mean "keep doing what you were doing". This understanding is essential for movement such as the back-up, where the reins should be the last factor in the movement, and the legs (and seat) the first. Ideally, the horse should continue backing up *without* increased rein pressure until your legs soften and your seat asks for a halt.

6. Lift the Back

A gentle heel or spur lifting action underneath the rib cage should encourage the horse to lift his back. Of course, this aid is used in conjunction with the seat and hands but the legs can be an effective motivator for the horse to lift his rib cage and "round" in the movement.

7. Lateral Movement

The positioning of your inside leg at the girth and outside leg behind the girth should combine to indicate a lateral movement. Where your seat goes and how your hands finish the movement will differentiate the shoulder-fore from the shoulder-in from the leg yield from the half-pass.

With the exception of the leg yield, your legs position in a way that encourages inside bend and catch the outside hind end (from swinging out). Finally, the horse will proceed to step in the direction of movement if that is required.

Give Up On Kicking!

Kicking your horse only stuns, disturbs, imbalances, and hurts. Although kicking might be a useful way to start out for a beginning rider, once you have better balance in your seat and a more consistent contact with the bit, aim toward using your legs with more purpose.

Learn how to use your legs in the rhythm of the movement. Working against the movement only serves to irritate the horse because he simply cannot respond if the timing is out of sync with the footfalls.

Good, effective leg aids work within the movement and are generally not noticeable. Great legs look like they are doing nothing at all. In all cases, the essential thing you need to do is to keep soft, loose legs draped gently on your horse's side. In this manner, the legs are kind, responsive, clear and secure. The horse knows he can rely on the communication he is receiving from the leg aids, and with repetition, will know just what to do when!

20 Why Would You Bother to "Scoop" Your Seat Bones?

We often talk about using our seat in horseback riding, but explaining exactly *how* to use the seat is not always explained in a clear manner. It's a difficult topic, but I'll take a stab at it. If nothing else, maybe the discussion here will motivate you to dive deeper into the topic with your instructor.

Why would you bother to learn to move the seat bones, you ask?

The seat is the most essential of all riding aids. Everything depends on the seat – your balance, your capacity to use your rein and leg aids, your coordination in following the horse's movements, even your ability to calm a nervous horse. Best of all, aiding from the seat can be the most effective form of communication you can have with your horse.

Without a deep, effective seat, your hands and legs will never become "independent" of the torso, and thereby they will always unintentionally interfere with the horse's movement.

The topic of the seat is long and complex. Learning to use your seat effectively should take a lifetime to develop, so we will begin with just one basic aspect: how to *move* the seat bones.

Well, it's simple but not so easy at the beginning.

Dining room chair - how did Kitty get in this picture?

Go Grab Your Dining Room Chair and Learn to Scoop

Do this off the horse: go grab one of those flat wooden chairs. Sit forward a bit on the edge of the chair, and work on tilting the chair forward so that it comes off its two back legs. The action required to get the chair to tilt is a "scooping" forward of the seat bones.

Can you tilt it with both seat bones? Can you tilt it with just one seat bone?

It may seem fairly easy to tilt the chair. Practice a bunch of times so your body can be blueprinted for the movement. Then, let's take that technique and head off to ride your horse. Now, you must scoop in the same way while the horse is moving!

On Horseback

When you are sitting on the horse, try for a moment to ignore your legs that are gently hanging on the horse's side. Keep your feet in the stirrups, but just let your legs hang and take your focus to your seat bones.

Ask the horse to walk and now, pretend that your seat bones take the place of your legs. In other words, start walking on your seat bones, in rhythm with the horse's movement. Use your seat bones as you would your legs – move them forward and backward as needed to follow the horse's stride.

If you want to walk on your seat bones, you have to "find the feel" of how to scoop forward and up with each seat bone at the right time. The trick is to identify which seat bone needs to move when. Scoop the left seat bone, then the right seat bone, then left-right-left-right and so on.

After you have tried this at the walk, try it at the sitting trot. The advantage of the trot is that it is only a two-beat movement and your seat bones can move forward together at the same moment (that you would have posted forward if you were posting). The disadvantage is that it is a quicker movement so your seat has to "scoop" forward/backward faster.

The canter has a serious scooping action. You might in fact have an easier time using your seat bones in the canter because it has a slower tempo (in general) and so you can follow easier and stay in the movement.

If you find your seat staying in the saddle more regularly, you know you're on the right track.

If you get tired after just a few minutes of riding, you know you're definitely on the right track!

If your horse suddenly snorts and loosens through the back, you can begin to celebrate!

21 Move to Stay Still on Horseback

It is true what they say – that horseback riders do nothing while the horse does all the work.

At least, that is what we all aspire to make it look like!

The best riders are the ones that make it look effortless – they glide along with their horses, always appearing to be in balance, making imperceptible movements that are barely evident except to the educated eye. Yes, the horse just flows from movement to movement seemingly on his own, as if he clearly knows what to do and where to do it.

But we know what it takes to get to that point. Years of riding and training go into developing the balance, strength and subtlety, never mind the amount of training the horse requires in order to be able to understand and respond to the slightest of aids.

How do we begin to look like we're sitting still, doing nothing on the horse's back?

We learn to move.

As with so many of life's paradoxes, only movement can make us appear to be still on our horses.

The reason: because the horse is moving.

If we truly stayed motionless on top of the horse (which would be nearly impossible due to the movement), we would be awkwardly jerking around in reaction to the horse's body position in the moment in time. Perhaps you've been there before? The horse lurches forward underneath you and you don't! Not only do you end up looking like you were *moving* on the horse, but it also feels uncomfortably like a mild whiplash.

However – if you learn to move in rhythm with the horse, suddenly, your body flows along in tandem with your equine partner. Within your constant movement, you create the illusion of being stable and unmoving.

What staying still *doesn't* look like

Don't make the mistake of floating along on top of the horse's back.

Many riders "perch" on their saddles. The horse flows along underneath the rider, but the rider has lifted her seat out of the saddle just enough that she is hovering above the movement. Her seat seems to be still but when the horse canters, she bounces in and out of the saddle. When in sitting trot, even if the horse is just trotting along steadily, the rider is holding herself outside of the movement, rather than becoming "one" with the forward/backward motion of the trot.

The major drawback to perching or hovering above the saddle is that should the horse take one unannounced step, the rider will be either left behind the movement or flung to the side. The rider will not be able to move *with* the horse in the misstep, and will risk becoming unseated or falling off.

The first essential aspect of sitting still – the independent seat

So long as the rider is relying on only hand or leg aids for balance and control, she will continue to be working outside of the horse's movement.

It's quite simple, really: the seat must belong to the horse. The difficult part is learning to move so that the seat *can* belong to the horse!

Where to start?

No blog (however wonderful!) and no book can give you the answer on how to use your seat effectively. (Un)fortunately, you must acquire the help of a competent instructor, and preferably, lunge lessons on a good horse. You need to learn to release your lower back and follow the horse's movements.

You have to develop your abdominals so that you can counter the sway in the canter – so your muscles can alternately release and contract to keep your upper body from leaning too far forward or back within the movement.

You must learn to move your seat bones independently of each other, and to be able to maintain soft but controlled legs that do not disturb your balance-in-movement. Once you have movement in the seat bones, you can begin to influence your horse's rhythm, bend, balance and engagement from the seat.

Sometime after developing the coordination needed to begin to ride *in* the horse, you will suddenly discover that you are looking more and more motionless. But you'll know how much you are in fact moving, within the movement!

22   Living (Horse) Life in the Basics

Although we revel in our various disciplines, riding and training styles and breeds of horses, there is simply no denying it: the basics are the basics and they are the same for us all. Can you distinguish the difference between good and bad movement?

Even if the you are unfamiliar with a discipline's competitive or technical requirements, chances are, you can tell if a performance was well done. The fact is that all movements share several components to them that are fundamental to the quality of movement. Despite our differences in riding style, we are all working toward the same basic purpose.

Rhythm Rules!

Every aspect of riding is rooted in rhythm. Without a sense of rhythm, all riding movements will be sabotaged and become relegated to a lurching, uneven-striding, uncertain series of steps, reducing our rides to a series of jolts, whip-lashed starts and stops, and tension in both the horse and rider.

Take the competitive trail horse, for example. When negotiating miles and miles of uneven terrain, there is no substitute for efficient, energy-saving movement. Whether at the walk, trot or canter, the gait must inevitably become regular to be non-taxing and economical.

Watch the hunter horse. The best mover is the one that masquerades as a metronome – each stride ticking away in an unwavering time measure. Anyone who has participated in a western trail pattern knows the essential dance that must occur in order to negotiate the obstacles in a smooth, cadenced manner.

I could go on and on, and cover all the disciplines I know of, and even those that I don't. The point is that rhythm is one of those commonalities that we all work toward.

Flexion

There are two types of flexion: longitudinal and lateral.
The first allows the horse to stretch over the topline and use his back effectively. The second allows side to side stretches. Both are essential to allow for soft, released movement that permits lighter strides and even use of musculature.

Flexion is what allows the horse to be supple left and right, and to lengthen or collect in movement. All figures, patterns and tricks require both kinds of flexion to be performed with ease and strength.

Go

This one is pretty self-explanatory.

Every aspect of riding horses begins with impulsion. The key is to have good enough communication with your horse so that he can put in the energy needed at the right time.

Here is an example. If you are heading into a corner with the horse trotting toward the arena walls, he will likely want to slow down to avoid hitting the wall. If uncorrected, you will teach your horse to "suck back", or lose energy, on every corner approach. Instead, you need to ride through the corner or turn with increased impulsion so that the horse can maintain the established rhythm. This is when a strong affinity to "go" enters the scene.

Imagine a barrel horse without "go".

What would a road horse be like without an easy ground-covering gait?

Contact/Connection

I might call it contact, and you might call it connection. It is the language that you and your horse share.

In the end, we are both talking about the same thing: the horse reaches to your aids – seat, weight, legs, hands and bit (or hackamore or whatever other kind of equipment) and there is a communication process that you both participate in. The better the connection, the more subtle the interaction.

The onlooker might only notice the *results* of the process – but you know how amazing it feels when the horse is "on the aids" and you progress together as one. Better yet is the confidence that your horse emanates because of your ease of communication.

Straightness

After finding bend and flexion, all horses must also discover the beauty of straightness.

Without body alignment, all movements lack strength and suppleness. The shoulders must be in line with the hips. The straighter the horse's body, the more efficient the movements become.

Moving straight, even on a circle, is a lifetime goal that is often difficult to achieve.

Collection

Many disciplines discuss the relatively complicated concept of collection. All higher level movements rely on it. Many of us claim to do it.

But don't be fooled! Most of us probably achieve "roundness" and confuse it with collection.

Collection is achieved only when all the above components are in place and practiced on a regular basis. True collection starts with a flexing of the joints in the hind end, a tilt of the haunches and a high level of activity that results in an elevated front end. When you first discover collection, you might be amazed at the energy surge and strength it takes to even begin to collect.

But if you look carefully, you will recognize it in many riding disciplines.

The most important aspect of all riding is to revisit the basic concepts and movements on a regular basis. No matter how many "buttons" your horse has, and how many cool moves you both can make, be sure to regularly check in with the above main goals. If you can maintain sound basics, the advanced movements will always be positively affected.

23 Top 10 Ways to Reward the Horse

As riders, we need to look for any excuse to celebrate our horse's achievements. Good riders are forever thankful for their equine's efforts as they push further stronger deeper and reach new heights. A happy horse is a willing partner, and many horses will give everything they have if they feel your acknowledgement and generosity of spirit.

Don't fool yourself.

Your horse knows exactly how you're feeling during the ride. They can "mind read" (more like body read) and know precisely when you are frustrated, upset, angry (?) and conversely, when you are relaxed, forgiving, joyful and ecstatic. We all know that positive reinforcement is as powerful a way to communicate as any other, and likely more appreciated by your four-legged friend.

Rewarding your horse doesn't have to be done on the ground with a treat in hand. In fact, encouragement received under saddle is more immediate and fulfilling than anything that is done on the ground after you ride. The key is to identify the right time to communicate your approval, and to know how to do it *in movement.*

So, without further discourse, here are ten simple ways to let your horse know he is on the right track.

10. **Think, "Yay/Wow/Great/Fantastic"** or whatever you feel at that moment, and be convinced that your horse can read your mind. Even though horses *can't* read minds, they can definitely read the involuntary messages your body sends through your seat, legs and hands – and they know if the thought was positive or negative. So yes, just *thinking* something nice will transfer seamlessly into your horse's mind.

9. **Say a soft, low "good" under your breath** so only he can hear it. You don't have to share your thank-you with the whole world; just say it loud enough for the horse's ears to flick back in your direction. Then watch as it goes forward again in appreciation.

8. **Pet your horse, b**ut DON'T smack him! Somewhere along the line, people thought smacking a horse was a good thing, and would be interpreted as such by the horse – it must be, since the horse is so big and strong, right? Well, now we know that the horse's skin is even more sensitive than human

skin. It stands to reason that a smack feels like a smack, and a pat or rub is a much more appreciated method.

7. Better yet, **slightly release your inside rein while you pet your horse** with your inside hand, in rhythm with the stride. Can you rub your belly and chew gum at the same time? Then this one is for you! While your horse is in motion, reach down lightly (but don't lean too far forward as you will change the horse's balance), and move your hand along the horse's neck in a forward/back movement, preferably in rhythm with the horse's head bob. Keep holding the same rein length through the petting action. This will release the inside rein while the neck is reaching forward/down, and then the contact will be gently taken up again by the time the neck comes back/up again.

The idea is not to interfere with the horse's movement, but to give a gentle inside rein release *while* petting the horse.

6. **Gently (very small movements) open and close your elbows in synch with the horse's body movements** – blend in with him so that he has freedom to swing his head and neck into the movement. You can give through both your elbows in order to move the hands and bit along with the horse. This will create a moment of harmony – no restriction, no instruction, no comment. Just follow along and encourage the horse to take a bolder forward stride thanks to less "stop" from the bit.

5. **Move a little bigger** into the movement of the horse. You always have the option of "releasing" with your seat: let your

lower back become loose and supple and follow along in an encouraging, enthusiastic manner – your horse will love the freedom in his back and just might reach further underneath himself with the hind legs in response.

4. *Hold your rein length* but **give a gentle half halt with an ending forward release** so your horse can stretch forward into the contact. In this manner, you can create a small space ahead of the horse that he can reach toward. If done diplomatically, a horse always appreciates feeling the slight freedom of extra space to move forward into.

3. **Stop asking for anything.** Sometimes, it is good enough to stop everything and just let the horse go along for a few strides. Beware – "stopping" doesn't mean that you suddenly drop everything and become a lumpy bumpy bag of jelly that causes the horse to fall to his knees! You can "stop" while maintaining the status quo – keep doing what you were doing, hold yourself strong and fluid, but just refrain from asking for anything *more* for the time being.

2. **Accept his idea.** Often, a horse will take initiative and offer something that you didn't ask for. Instead of correcting or changing what he did, just ride along for a moment. You can get back to your topic in a few strides, but teaching the horse to take initiative, especially in the early stages of your riding relationship or when the horse is young, can go far to developing a great rider/horse rapport in the long run.

1. **Do your horse's favourite movement**. All horses have preferred movements that get them all excited! For example,

my gelding loves the stretchy trot or canter – he snorts and reaches and the ears flick forward. My mare gets jazzed up with the flying change – again, rambunctious snorts, perky ears, and expression in her face and overall body outline. Find out what your horse's favourite movement is, and then do it at the end of a session or after something difficult!

The sooner you can reinforce your horse's actions, the sooner he will connect the reward to the desired behaviour. Be light, quick and to the point. Then, go onto the next part of your ride. Look for more to celebrate as you transition into the next movement.

Most importantly, *reward quickly and often.*

Read on to the next chapter for even more ideas.

24 The Need for "Yes" Speed – While You Ride Your Horse

There are more ways than one to let your horse know his efforts are appreciated and he is on the right track. Just as you need positive reinforcement, your horse needs to know that he can find his "happy place" while you are on his back.

The two tried and true methods of petting the horse and saying "good" certainly help to communicate your positive message. But did you know that there are many other more subtle ways you can say "yes?"

The Need for "Yes" Speed

As you develop in your riding skills, you will begin to recognize the ongoing physical communication you have with your horse during your ride. This communication goes much deeper than a verbal discussion we can have with our human friends.

Better balance and "quieter" aids will enable you to realize that...

... communication between rider and horse occurs as quickly as we can think – actually, no. It happens even faster than that.

Because we are literally connected to our horse through our seat and legs, our "discussion" speed can happen as quickly as our central nervous system can respond to the horse's movements. In the long run, we might become even faster in our discussion than we can think (thereby leaving the "thinking" moments for when we are off the horse's back).

Another reason you want to say "yes" quicker than speaking or petting is that things can happen very quickly on a horse's back. So while you are flying off to the left riding through a buck, you might want to be saying, through your body language, "Stop the buck – GOOD!" *instantly*. Many a horse will find relaxation and security in the rider than can follow them in their language pattern and speed.

When you can communicate this quickly through your aids, the onlooker will not have any inkling about the many and varied messages being sent back and forth between you and your horse.

However, the experienced onlooker might notice the tell-tale sign: an active yet calm horse working enthusiastically in sync with his rider. And of course, the rider appears to be doing nothing.

So how can you say "yes" quickly enough to help guide your horse effectively and efficiently *while you ride*?

9 Ways to Say "Yes" While Riding

1. Release through the inside rein.

That inside rein is the maker or breaker of the inside hind leg. This means that it also affects the horse's balance pretty much all the time. So if you can find an excuse to give a little "yes" through the rein, you will discover a significant method that communicates comfort and strength to the horse. He will appreciate being able to bring his hind leg underneath his body so that he can balance both you and himself better.

2. Release through your seat.

The seat release is almost as powerful as the inside rein release. While you ride, you can either brace your seat, become passive or actively release. Most of the seat control comes through your lower back, which communicates your messages to your horse through his back. So if things are going well, you can let loose through your lower back so that you can synchronize your movement with the horse's swing.

3. Softening of the legs/knees.

We often grip tighter than we need to with both the knees and the legs. When you want to communicate harmony with your horse, try softening through your calves and even your knees. Work on lengthening your legs from the hip so that there is only a soft angle in your knees, and your legs can therefore "drape" along your horse's sides.

4. Opening of the seat.

This is a little different than the seat release. When you open, you in effect create an open space to invite the horse into as he is moving. So if you want to do a leg yield to the right, you can encourage with a "yes" when the horse steps right by actually opening the right seat bone in rhythm to the right direction. This is tricky but the results can be awe-inspiring.

5. Stretchy walk/trot break.

Ah! The stretchy! Once a horse learns to release his topline into an active stretch, he will always look forward to a stretch in either walk or trot.

6. Do his favorite move.

Most horses have a favorite romp that makes them happy and lets them know that things are just great. Find out what your horse likes best and let him play once in a while after a particularly challenging maneuver.

7. Celebratory hand gallop.

Teach the horse to "stride out" when things go well. So instead of slowing down to a walk or halt, go for a run! Amp things up, get hot and sweaty and hear the wind whistle in your ears! You might be surprised to realize how much your horse likes this once he knows he is allowed to stretch out once in a while!

8. Lighten through the seat and body.

Do you remember how you used to be able to jump up into a loved one's arms as a child? You could hold yourself in a way that allowed them to hold you up for a long time because you were holding your own body tone to help them out. In the same manner, you can control how heavy your body feels to the horse. Say "yes" by lightening through your seat, holding your torso in a more toned manner and allowing the horse to have a bit more freedom underneath you as you ride.

9. Flowing through your body with the horse's movement.

This is the most important "yes" you can give your horse. If you can follow through not only your seat, but through your whole body, commit to the movement and "be there", you are able to give the strongest "yes" communication possible. And this can be done instantaneously, long before you can even open your mouth to say the word "good!"

So there you have it! Next time you ride, try some of these tips and see what your horse says.

25　Do You Make This Timing Mistake?

Have you ever given your horse an aid and received nothing in return? Perhaps your horse simply didn't respond? You did it again, and nothing resulted even the second time.

Perhaps your horse gave you an unwanted response – did he pin his ears, scramble forward or even throw out a little buck or kick?

Most of us would then repeat the aid, and expect the horse to "learn" the correct response, because after all, it is the horse that needs to understand what we are doing, and not the other way around!

If you ever find yourself in a vicious cycle with the horse not improving and possibly deteriorating in response, there could be one other variable that you might not have considered – the *TIMING* of the aid.

The timing of the aid has to do with everything – time it wrong, and you might as well be doing nothing, or worse still, irritating your horse.

Every gait has an inherent rhythm to it. You can probably already feel the "swing" of the horse's back in that gait. You might know how to post and/or sit rhythmically in the trot, and follow the canter gently through your seat so you don't smack the horse's back with each stride. You can easily use your seat and leg aids and steadily, with feeling, use your hands to keep the energy "recycling" back into the horse rather than let it all out the front.

For the most part, your horse is quite pleased with your riding skills! But you know that you and your horse are not yet "one" – there is something missing that prevents you from moving together in tandem – the type of communication that makes onlookers think that you can read each other's mind.

Breaking Down the Stride

Simply put, the horse cannot respond to your aid if the inside hind foot is on the ground.

Once that foot lands on the ground, it is immobilized and unable to do anything other than bear weight. The time to use an aid is when that foot is heading *off* the ground into the air.

"Not" Moment: Aiding at this point in the right lead canter stride would only irritate or confuse the horse.

You need to energize the leg as it is cycling through the air into the next stride. Your aid window is only that one moment when the horse is able to reach further underneath the body, or take a lateral step, or change gait.

The moment resurfaces every time the horse takes the inside hind leg off the ground, but it is there only for that moment!

Canter Moment: Aiding should have already been applied as the left (inside) hind leg is lifting off the ground.

You have to find that space in time and make it useful. Applying an aid should be done in rhythm within those moments – stride by stride rather than maintained steadily through several strides. You may find yourself, in effect, *dancing* your aids to the horse, in the rhythm that works best for him.

It may sound complicated to time your aids, but it really isn't too difficult. Rather than having to focus on the inside hind leg (which can be difficult if you haven't developed the "feelers" in your seat), you can look to the inside front leg for a clue as to what the inside hind leg is doing.

Trot Moment: In this moment, the left (inside) hind leg is preparing to lift off the ground. The left front leg (and right hind) is going to be weight bearing.

How to Time Your Aids

Walk or Trot: Apply your aids when the inside front leg is on its way back.

Canter: Apply your aid when the horse is in the "down stride" of the canter

In both examples, the inside hind leg would be in the moment of elevation. Should you apply the aid in that moment, the inside hind leg would be able to respond as it is still gliding through the air.

That is all there is to it! Pay close attention, wait for the moment, execute the aid during the non-weight bearing stride, and let the horse respond.

Try it and see if it makes a difference to your horse's ability to respond!

26 First, Plan Your Ride. Then, Be Ready to Scrap It.

Has this ever happened to you?

You know exactly what you want to do during your ride. Your horse is prepped, you have all the gear you need, and you head to the riding ring with high hopes and a set plan. You get on, get going, and then discover that your horse has something entirely different in mind!

At this point, you have two choices: keep going with what you were planning to do, or scrap it and work on what your horse *needs* to work on.

Goal Setting: Step-by-Step Development

You need to know what you want to do during a ride. There is nothing worse than wandering around and around in circles, aimlessly pounding legs into sand for little purpose other than perhaps a little conditioning for the horse.

There is no replacement for goal setting in the quest for improvement in riding. When you have an idea of the path you want to take, and the skills you want to develop, it is always good to plan out what you want to do before you get on the horse's back. Each ride should be a development from the last, setting up a series of successes for (yourself and) your horse as he progresses in his training and education.

What are you going to work on today? What went well last ride, what would you like to develop, and what movements will your horse enjoy? How will you warm up? What is the "lesson" for today? How will you cool down? Make your time count, make it a quality ride and then get off.

Be clear on the basic skills your horse needs, develop them toward the next level and then finally (over the course of a number of years), move up to the highest levels of training in your discipline.

When to Scrap the Plan

However, goal setting can only take you so far. Even though you are inspired to get that horse to do the next cool thing, your horse might simply not be ready.

Alternately, he might be able to do some parts of the new movement, but loses the basic, most fundamental aspects to riding – enough that the movement becomes labored, difficult and unappealing. Maybe the horse puts up a fuss and even quits.

This is when you should scrap your grand ideas, and get back down to the business of the basics. Many of the basic movements, like maintaining rhythm, looseness, or the simple act of moving forward, are integral to all levels of riding and therefore should be worked on regularly even if you are also working on something else at the same time.

It is much more important to develop solid basics – regardless of how advanced your horse is. Have the patience and awareness to re-establish the important aspects of movement.

Because the basics are where it's at. Without the fundamental skill set, there will never be soft, fluid, responsive, *enthusiastic* work from your horse.

27   Quit to Persevere

Learning a new skill in riding can be pretty daunting. Not only do you need to coordinate your entire body (including the ever-pervasive 'core' of your body), but you also need to stay in balance *while moving, in time*, in partnership with the (much larger) horse that happens to be using his own feet while yours are dangling in mid-air! You get my drift....

So at best, it's not easy. When other people tell you that riding is all about the horse and not about the rider, you can be fairly sure that they have never sat on a horse to know what it really feels like. Even with the best horse, at the very least, the rider has to "get out of the way" and to do THAT can be a feat in itself!

Assuming that you have the most willing horse, it may be that your own body simply cannot put all the tiny components together at the same time, at the *right* time, because unfortunately, it's not only about the physical coordination of skill, it's also about timing within the moment of stride that makes it easiest for the horse to respond. And so communication might break down even with the best interests in mind.

One of the first 'life lessons' that all of us riders learn from our horses is to persevere. Our mantra is "try, try again." "Keep at it." If we give in to the doom and gloom of the moment, we'll never accomplish anything. Maybe one of the repetitions will yield a wanted outcome. Maybe if you do it enough times, your horse will *finally* get it. Right?

Wrong.

Although repeating the aids and 'sticking with the program' is useful many times, there may come a day when you could repeat the exercise a thousand times to no avail – and end up frustrating both yourself and your horse.

So what are some alternatives?

- Change the topic. Go to something else, 'let it go', and come back to it later in the same riding session.

- Try again – just be sure to control your emotion and reward even the smallest effort in the right direction.

- Quit. Put it to rest. Be done with it. (Did I just say that??)

Yes – there is nothing wrong with 'giving up'. In my many (not saying quite how many!) years of riding, one thing the horses have taught me is that they have no problem with dropping the subject today and picking it up again tomorrow.

Just make sure that you finish the ride on a good note. You do NOT have to finish on a 'perfect' note in regards to the skill you were building – you just need to go to something that makes you both happy and confident – and finish.

Then come back to it the next day. You'll find that your horse went and did his 'homework' and maybe, just maybe, your coordination (muscle memory) is a tiny bit better. Just keep at it – persevere not by drilling on and on, but by giving yourself permission to quit.

28 What To Do When Your Horse Isn't Being Cute

There is something special and attractive about a horse's magnificence and grace, his beautiful eyes and even his smell – at least, for those of us who are "horse crazy." We are often so taken by his beauty and presence that we overlook his herd animal mentality. Instead, we interpret his actions through humanizing eyes that explain away their actions in sometimes less than accurate ways.

You have probably seen it so many times – the horse being pushy and the handler either letting the behavior go or honestly not being aware of the problem.

The horse might paw. He might perk up his ears and give us a loving look for more treats. Or he might nod his head up and down. Maybe he pulls away while being led. Sometimes, he might nibble on your hat or hair.

At the very least, it can become irritating. At the worst, it's unsafe for both horse and handler. The most serious consequence is when the behavior escalates and problems develop. Then suddenly, what was cute becomes dangerous and people and horses get hurt.

If the horse owner isn't aware of what the horse is truly communicating, then the risk increases for both human and horse.

Understanding The Language of Horses

The number one rule for all things "horse" is safety. In all circumstances, the horse's sheer size is reason enough for us to set guidelines for our interactions with horses, and to follow them to the letter. Any time we bend the rules, or let the little things slip by, not only do we become inconsistent in our interactions with our horses (and therefore "lying" to them), but we also increase the physical risks to ourselves and to those around our horses.

The biggest problem is when someone misinterprets the horse's intentions and ascribe "herd-naughty" behavior as being something cute. The mistake isn't in the interpretation itself; it is that the person is indicating to the horse that the behavior is acceptable.

Although they might be unaware of the language of horses, by not responding to the behavior, the person is assuming a subservient role.

Knowing when a horse communicates dominating behavior is the first step toward becoming a responsible horse owner. Once we know what the horse is saying, we begin to learn how to respond and eventually prevent the conditions that allow for such thoughts to go through our horses' minds.

What To Do

Your response does not need to be harsh or punishing. You can approach these situations from an educational perspective. Every situation is an opportunity to train your horse. Try to identify what works without causing the horse to lose confidence in you.

Stay calm, be confident and consistent in your responses. You must demonstrate your leadership skills in order to gain the respect of the horse. Once the horse knows that he can respect (and therefore trust) his humans, he will happily assume a following role.

In the end, it is our responsibility to make sure the horse understands what is expected of him. If we either willfully ignore or really and truly don't know how to teach acceptable behavior for horse-human interactions, we can be setting up conditions that can one day escalate into seriously dangerous situations.

What NOT to do:

Don't get mad.
Don't get even.
Don't lose your cool.

Although these are just suggestions, remember that there is rarely a need to get mad and become physically aggressive to get a result. Stay calm, be purposeful and most especially, be consistent.

*****Please always remember: when working with, on or around horses, always make decisions that ensure your safety as well as the horse's. If in doubt, back off and re-evaluate before things escalate.*****

Pawing

Horse Speak Definition: In general, pawing is a sign of impatience or anxiety. The horse wants to move.

What To Do: If the horse is being held by a handler (for example, in a show environment), then by all means, allow the horse to go for a walk. Better yet, use the energy to teach or perfect something while the horse is walking. Try getting the horse to step away from you as he is walking. Can he cross his legs (front only, back only, both front and back) while he is walking?

Walking off might not be suitable in all situations. If the horse is in cross-ties in the barn, you can still easily stop the pawing by picking one foot and asking it to step forward/back/ forward/back until the horse is ready to stop moving.

Then give the horse the opportunity to stop. If he isn't ready to stop, go to it again!

Head Nodding

Horse Speak Definition: Head nodding is also another sign of excess energy or tension.

What To Do: Change the topic and do some of the same things suggested for pawing. Always aim to get the horse to step away from you rather than step into you so that you demonstrate your leadership to him (and stay safe).

Pushing you out of the way

Horse Speak Definition: This one can become very dangerous since every time the horse gets you to move away from him, he will become more and more convinced of his leadership over you.

As you may notice in any turn-out field, the dominant horse usually gets his way and tells all the other horses what to do and where to go. Becoming the secondary citizen in your herd of two may not suit you well since you are also one-sixth the size of the horse and can be very easily hurt!

What To Do: Once again, be sure to assert your leadership. Decide on a personal space "bubble" around you that the horse should not enter.

Then, before the horse steps into that space, push him out – first, with your body language (step into his space) and if he does not respond to that social cue, then follow through by pushing him away with the lead rope or bridle reins.

He must never get closer to you, even while walking beside you, than what you've decided is a safe personal space around you.

Dragging you along on the lead

Horse Speak Definition: This often happens when something else (other than you) requires much more urgent attention of the horse. He is knowingly or unknowingly disregarding your communications and going where he needs to go (iften toward his herd mates).

What To Do: This behavior is the opposite of the one above. Should your horse drag you, do your best to stop and assume one position. Then swing his head around in a way that makes him turn to face you. Maybe you can back him up a few steps after he stops and looks at you. Maybe you ask him to step sideways away from you for a set number of footfalls.

Try walking ahead after you feel he is softly compliant. If he goes to drag you off again, go back to moving his feet where you want them to go. In all cases, do not allow him to continue taking *you* for a walk! Treat this behavior seriously as there is great danger of you getting hurt.

Nibbling on your hat or hair

Horse Speak Definition: Isn't it so cute when your horse reaches forward with a lovingly stretched out neck and gently nibbles on your hair or hat? NO!

Again, in the herd, the dominant horse is the one that does the nibbling. Please be assured that what you think of as being cute is a completely different message to the horse: that he is boss and you should do what he says.

What To Do: This one is easy to prevent – just don't tempt him with your hat, hair, or anything else for that matter! Stay out of his nibbling zone and consistently establish your personal space bubble.

Begging for treats

Horse Speak Definition: As humans, we get a pleasure rush when we do something nice for someone else. We especially enjoy sharing meals and treats together – sharing food is simply in our nature.

Unfortunately, herd dynamics don't follow human social norms. The only time one horse gives another horse food (or gets out of the way) is when the second horse is dominant over the first.

Every time you give a treat to your horse, you are communicating to him that he is the leader in your herd of two. This might not be a problem for some time, but should your normally gentle and sweet horse start becoming demanding and pushy, you can blame it on the repeated communication you've been giving him.

What To Do: One option is to refrain from ever giving your horse treats by hand. Some people always stick to this rule. If you must hand feed treats, be sure to avoid giving the treat at the first sign of aggressive behavior from your horse.

Establish clear parameters and be consistent. If in doubt, go back to option 1!

Stomping feet or turning your way when you touch an area

Horse Speak Definition: The horse is uncomfortable for some reason and is making it clear that you should get out of his space.

What To Do: First, find out if there is truly a physical discomfort. Perhaps you will need a veterinarian to check the horse and see if there is a problem with that area.

If it is likely that the horse is being aggressive, then look to either change the behavior (redirect the energy and get the horse to move specific feet, as in pawing and head nodding above) or simply push the horse out of your personal space. Make it clear that you can move his feet and assume the leader position in the "herd" dynamic.

In all the above examples, the key thing to remember is that the horse doesn't know any better. He is simply communicating to you in the way he knows how. It is your duty to understand "horse speak" and negotiate through all the herd dynamic social rules. The better you understand the "horse" definitions behind your actions, the quicker you will be in knowing how to prevent unwanted behavior, and knowing what to do about it.

Section 3: The Training
~ Getting Deeper Into The Basics

29   Muscle Memory Matters in Horse Riding

Malcolm Gladwell put forth a theory in 2008, in his book, *Outliers: The Story of Success* that sounds to be entirely relevant to us horse riders. In it, he proposes that it takes 10,000 hours of practice in any task to become exceptionally good at something.

That breaks down to approximately 3 hours per day over a course of ten years. He goes on to explain that it's not just about having talent – less talented people can progress beyond their more talented counterparts through repeated, directed practice.

Another key component to his theory is that one must be in the right place, at the right time, in order to achieve one's highest potential for success. In the horse sense, I have always thought of this as being influenced by the right people at the right time – preferably very early in your riding career so that the correct muscle memory can be created early (we know how hard it is to undo bad habits – especially physical ones!).

Although not everyone agrees with Gladwell's theory, and the criticism is that he makes broad generalizations based on a relatively small amount of data, I suspect there is something to be said about regular practice. It does not take a genius to recognize that repeating a skill tends to develop the skill.

This could be especially relevant to riding horses, as there are so many small muscle contractions that act within split-seconds in order for us to keep ourselves in the saddle and moving in tandem with the horse. Anyone who has ridden for even a short time can attest to the development of 'muscle memory', or blueprinting.

Things just become easier with practice. Once upon a time you thought you'd never be able to perform a movement, but with regular determined repetition, one day you discover that it just happens. Somehow, you do not even have to think about the movement and your body just performs.

Yes, I imagine that if I could squeeze in three hours of riding a day, I would get to my goal of being efficient and effective in the saddle much quicker. This certainly holds true for riding, as well as anything in life, including success at our daily jobs.

On the horse side of the equation, I have one particularly expressive horse who has distinctly TOLD me that this theory stands true for horses as well. He is the one that thrives on daily *anything* (insert riding, grooming, tail brushing, lunging – you name it) and if it happens that he gets a day or two off, he emphatically denies that he has ever been ridden. He tells me his slow and fast twitch muscle fibers have absolutely no memory of ever having twitched that way before...!

I guess the moral of this story is to just get out there – and go for a ride! Start packing away those hours.

30 Blueprinting – the Good, the Bad, the Ugly

Riding is a whole-body endeavour that involves every part of the rider. From controlling the tips of the fingers to the ends of the toes to everything in between, the body must be engaged in large and small movements over space in time. Aids must be precise and timed in relation to the horse's movement. At any given moment, the rider must be engaged in some expression of movement in order to follow and guide the horse's next steps.

Blueprinting, in the riding sense, refers to the muscle memory that is developed in both the horse are rider. The whole concept of riding could seem to be a very daunting task if it weren't for the fact that muscles develop a movement 'blueprint' – once the neural pathways are engaged and connected, similar movements in similar circumstances become easier and easier until that particular movement occurs with little conscious thought.

In effect, with sufficient practice, the rider can stop having to think about what the body is doing – she can essentially send the body on auto-pilot and think very little other than to get down to the business of 'feeling'.

The Good

Blueprinting is an advantage in the sense that once you achieve 'autopilot' you can rely on your central nervous system (CNS) to do most of the 'thinking' in response to the many tiny movements required to respond to the horse's movements.

The time it takes to send messages to brain and then instructions back to the body is too long to be able to keep up fluidly with the horse's movements. Letting the CNS take over allows you to release your muscles and joints so they can easily flow with the horse.

When you reach this state of non-thinking, you can begin to ride more in the right brain, and start riding with "feel".

Then the magic happens – you no longer feel earthbound – your horse floats along with ease and the rules of gravity seem to no longer apply. Similarly, your horse resonates with bliss – with snorts, soft floppy ears, and effortless flow of the back.

For all intents and purposes, it appears as if you and your horse are moving 'as one', thinking the same thought, dancing the dance.

The Bad

The bad news about blueprinting is that the same learning process occurs with all body movements – even the ones you'd rather NOT duplicate! We usually consider these movements to be bad habits, things we know we are doing but we shouldn't be doing!

The trouble with blueprinting in the negative sense is that the undesired movement becomes the 'autopilot' movement and so a vicious cycle begins to reproduce itself. And the biggest obstacle comes when you try to *undo* the physical movement and try to replace it with something more suitable.

Now, you have to THINK about each aspect of the new movement – and tell each part of your body to make that movement one step at a time... which in general, ends up being too slow to correspond to the horse's movement. The re-education process takes much time and effort – in fact, much more effort to undo than if it was correctly learned in the first place.

The Ugly

Worse still, is when you are so permanently blueprinted that you don't even recognize that you are producing an unwanted movement. It becomes unconscious, and your body effectively begins to lie to you – you think you're doing one thing when in fact, you're doing something else. In this case, it becomes difficult to even identify what is causing the situation, never mind try to find a solution.

What to do?

It seems that the situation is pretty daunting. What is a rider to do, especially because everything we do in the saddle influences the horse, either positively or negatively? The obvious answer is to get the right blueprinting in the first place. Your first riding experiences can set the stage either way – for the good or the bad.

The key, as always, is to find a good riding instructor. Also, find a good "school master" – a horse that is well trained, good minded and reliable, so he can teach you. Progress on to younger/less educated/more sensitive horses only after you have developed sufficient skills and then, keep getting guidance from a good instructor.

For those of us who are already not-perfectly-blueprinted: be ready to buckle up the seat belt and stay for the long haul. It will take time, patience and perseverance. Be forgiving of both yourself and your horse. Ride with a kind sense of humour. Be satisfied with small steps in the right direction. Know when to quit, and when to try again. Stay determined, but stay gentle and calm. Enjoy the path, and don't be too quickly discouraged. And above all else, listen to your horse, for if you can hear, you will get all the answers you need to succeed.

31   Bend: How to Drift Out on Purpose

It is true that we regularly deliberate about the evils of overusing the inside rein.

It is also true that we constantly discuss the importance of the horse responding to your outside aids and how they regulate the impulsion, speed and bend of the horse.

But there is a time that it is perfectly fine, or almost advisable, for you to allow the horse to drift to the outside, seemingly contradicting all rational reasoning.

When It's OK To Let Your Horse Drift Out

Have you ever found yourself heading into an ever-decreasing spiral after a sudden sideways step to the inside? Maybe your horse spooked momentarily and did an exit-stage-left – at which point, you fell into the turn with him and almost encouraged the turn to become a tighter-tighter circle that left you unseated and both of you confused.

Or maybe you were indicating a mild turn or heading into a corner, but your horse misinterpreted your aids into thinking that he should drop the inside shoulder and "fall in", thereby reducing the arc of the circle you were intending to follow.

Or your efforts to create an inside bend were met with a braced jaw and heavy weight on the rein.

In any case, you felt a stiffness on the inside aids. You knew that just going with the flow was not conducive to maintaining balance, but you went along because there was seemingly not much else that could be done.

The "Drift-Out"

Letting the horse escape ever so slightly to the outside might be just what you need in those moments.

Although we do go on and on about keeping a strong outside rein and leg aids, a brief softening of the outside aids might be just the ticket to allow your horse to shift his weight from the inside to the outside. Use a corresponding inside leg to support the horse's rib cage, and you might find him stepping away from the inside leg, softening on the inside rein and balancing more to the outside (which would then begin to even out his balance).

If you dressage readers think that this sounds suspiciously like a leg yield, you'd be right!

The difference here is that you'd be doing a leg yield on a turn or circle, not just on a straight line.

Similar to the straight leg yield, the legs should cross and the body moves to the outside. However, in the drift-out, you might actually encourage the horse to take a deeper bend through the body.

After all, you are on a turn or a circle, and a bend is necessary to allow the horse's inside hind leg to come deeper underneath the body. During a turn, the leg can support the horse's balance better and successfully counteract the force of gravity.

The Aids

It is always better to begin the aids before the horse has fully committed his weight to the inside.

1. Start with your inside leg and seat. In the rhythm of the gait, push both toward the outside of the circle or turn.

2. Maintain or if possible, soften the pressure on the inside rein. Be sure you are not pulling back.

3. Soften (but do not completely release) the outside rein and leg aids.

4. Encourage or allow the horse to step to the outside, crossing the legs within the rhythm of the gait.

5. Do this for two to four strides. You might need to repeat this exercise several times to benefit from it. However, it is not necessary to drift out for too many steps in a row, as it is a correction and not a way of going.

Good signs

You know you're on the right track if your horse increases the depth of his bend with less effort. He might lighten up on the inside rein. His rib cage might actually shift back in alignment with the body and certainly, the leaning pressure on your inside leg will be alleviated.

You might notice that the outside rein "fills up" with the bend of the neck and that there is a place for your outside leg to lie comfortably against.

You will probably feel the shift of the weight to the outside.

Maybe your own seat will feel more evenly balanced over the center of the horse.

*****

Once you get good at drifting out, you will find a bend quicker and with less effort. You might want to explore the same idea in all the gaits, including the canter.

As with any correction, too much of a good thing might not make it great. Too much drifting out will result in the horse not responding to the outside aids, becoming crooked to the outside.

In that case, you could try a counter-bend and drift in! The exact same principles would apply in the opposite way. But this can be a topic for another day.

32 How to "Fill Up" Your Outside Rein for a True Neck Rein

"Use your outside rein!"

"You need a better neck rein so you can balance the horse better."

"Half-halt/check with the outside rein."

In any of these three scenarios, your instructor is letting you know that your outside rein is either not being used correctly, or it isn't active enough to be helping your horse. However, a neck rein isn't an outside rein that is simply pulled backward.

We often rely so much on our inside rein that we tend to forget the purpose and use of the outside rein. We can apply the outside rein as a direct rein, or a neck rein. Although both work to achieve better balance and

154

communication with the horse, there are significant differences to each. In this chapter, we will talk about why and how to create an effective neck rein.

We use the neck rein in all disciplines. Regardless of the style of riding, the neck rein can and should be used for basic communication. Using a snaffle bit, the outside rein is generally shorter and used with contact. Using a curb bit, the rein is longer and ideally used with less contact. However, in general, the neck rein is used in the same manner in all disciplines and for the same purposes.

What Is A Neck Rein?

This specific type of rein aid is identified by the way that it "wraps around" the outside of the horse's neck. In general, it sits gently along the horse's neck and is always available to act within the right moment in the horse's stride.

Why Use A Neck Rein?

The neck rein acts as a powerful communicator. Used with contact, it can help the horse maintain balance by half-halting the energy as it comes to the forehand. Too much energy left unchecked will cause the horse to fall forward onto the front legs. The neck rein can prevent the fall before it happens and help the horse maintain more weight on the hind legs. In this manner, when used at the end of a sequence of aids, the outside neck rein is a main actor in creating and maintaining collection.

Drifting out on purpose (leg yield on a circle) allows the horse to develop a better bend, which then helps to create a neack rein.

Once you become more adept in using your body aids, the neck rein also can become the initiator of a turn. Rather than pulling on the inside rein, the horse learns to *move away* from the neck rein.

So if you want to turn left, you apply the right neck rein and use your seat/leg/torso aids to indicate the direction. The horse feels the "wrapped around the neck" rein pressure and steps away from it.

This way, you can limit the use of the inside rein to just maintaining flexion (so that you can see the corner of the horse's inside eye). The by-product of less inside rein is that you will not restrict the inside hind leg from reaching as far as it should to balance around the turn.

"Filling Up" the Neck Rein

I use the term filling up because the neck rein isn't about just pulling backward. In fact, the ideal situation is to hold the rein at the desired length you need for the moment, and then to "push" the horse into the rein. The horse steps toward the rein, feels the pressure and then responds.

- Use your inside aids to bend the horse.

Starting with your weight on your inside seat bone, then leg, then upper body, push the horse to the outside of the circle. As your horse gets better, and your timing gets better, your push will become lighter. But at the beginning, you may need a fair amount of pressure to be clear in what you want.

- Inside rein is for flexion.

The only thing your inside rein should do is to maintain the flexion in the horse's head – that is, to keep the horse looking to the inside of the turn. Otherwise, it should be softly fluttering in and out of contact as needed. What it shouldn't be doing is maintaining a rigid pressure on the horse's mouth.

- Maintain a steady outside rein

If you can keep your outside rein at a consistently "good" length (depending on your discipline), you will begin to feel the horse as he steps to the outside, thereby filling up the outside rein.

At this point, you will have the neck rein positioned and the horse stepping into it. Now, it is up to you to use it to your advantage. As mentioned above you can use it to rebalance the horse, or use it to initiate a turn. As your horse begins the turn, you can keep the neck rein in light contact, being fairly inactive, unless you need to as again.

Once you discover the power of the neck rein, you'll wonder how you ever rode without it. Using an effective neck rein is one more step in the direction of becoming more subtle and harmonious with your horse. Not only that, but it will also allow him to move with a straighter body and spine.

33   Four Steps to Help Your Horse Through a Turn

I'm sure you've seen it before – there are many situations where a horse turns too abruptly, unbalancing himself and also the rider. Most often, the rider hangs on but other times, she might be unseated, losing balance, stirrups and/or seat.

It happens when the horse turns too soon, cutting the arc of the circle so small that he has to catch himself with his front legs in order to avoid a fall. It can happen in the hunter/jumper ring especially after a jump, on a dressage 20m circle, on a reining or horsemanship pattern or on a trail that winds its way through the forest.

Regardless of the situation, there are several ways to help the horse through the turn. By being an active rider, you can:

1. predict the lean into the turn
2. support before the horse loses balance

3. teach the horse to reach straight through the turn

4. release (lighten contact and follow the horse with your seat) as soon as possible.

Let's take a closer look at each step.

Predict the Lean

You know it's coming! So instead of waiting for it to happen and THEN trying to do something about it after the horse is off balance, prepare several strides ahead of time. Shorten your reins if they've become too long (but keep the bend in your elbows). Sit tall in the saddle. Use your inside leg more actively *before* the lean. Keep the horse's neck straight (although the head can slightly flex in the direction of the turn).

Support

Use an active seat, leg and reins to lightly carry the horse several strides past the point where he wanted to lean. Your legs and seat can act as a wall that prevents your horse's rib cage from leaning. You might need a stronger inside rein if the horse is travelling with his head and neck flexed to the outside. You might need a stronger outside rein if the horse is swinging his head to the inside. In any case, keep your horse's neck aligned with his body.

Half-halt once, twice, or several times, at the right time, in order to help rebalance the horse's weight to the hind end.

For the horse that rushes, slow his leg speed. For the horse that slows down, ask for more from the hind end.

Straighten

Even though you are on a turn, the horse does not have to feel like he has to scramble through it with a tight, tense body. Break down your turn into a number of straight strides, and ask your horse to go straight longer, and turn for less strides. Imagine that your turn or circle is a hexagon, with many short straight lines attached together.

Find all the straight lines in the circle. Then ride the turn that way.

Make sure you are not leaning into the turn yourself. We often lean without even knowing it. Stay tall, stay straight with your own seat and shoulders, and follow the arc of the turn at the right moment.

Take as many strides as needed to make a better balanced, more controlled turn when you finally ask for it.

Release

Well, this doesn't mean throw the reins away. It does mean that you can stop resisting through your body and flow with the horse. You can lighten the rein contact and encourage the horse to reach forward with a bold stride or two. It also means that he can find his balance once again in preparation for the next turn or movement.

Helping a horse through a turn might take many repetitions before the horse can more easily maintain better balance. It is often more tempting to give in to gravity than to carry one's weight with strength and agility. But it can be done.

Once the horse has better understanding, you will notice that he becomes less tense as he nears a turn. You might feel that he begins to swing through the back better, become bouncier in his gait and maybe even take bolder steps with his hind legs coming further underneath the body.

**Maintaining balance through a turn
takes practice and preparation.**

He might snort, soften through the poll and ears, and generally give you a feel-good message.

You will also have an easier time because you can maintain better balance and prepare for the next movement up ahead. And the onlooker will see a horse that calmly but boldly negotiates a smooth, easy turn without fuss or scramble, appearing to be so athletic that he *could* turn on a dime – if he wanted to!

34   Why You Must Shoulder-Fore Your Horse on the Rail and How To Do It

The shoulder-fore is the like the little sibling that always plays second fiddle to the shoulder-in. But don't discount its power. When left to themselves, most horses will travel crookedly up a line. In fact, they may also be crooked on circles.

On a straight line, they tend to lean outward toward the rail with their front end. So, if you watch a horse go up a rail from behind, you will clearly see the front end traveling on a line closer to the rail, while the hind end drifts somewhat off the rail. There might be a tendency for the horse's head and neck to point outward, away from the direction of travel. So if the horse is going right, the head and neck point left.

On circles, they tend to bend to the outside going one way. Let's say your horse has a natural bend to the left. So going right, he will continue to bend to the left. That is, he points to the outside of the turn. Going left will be different. Because of his natural crookedness, he will tend to overbend in the direction that he is naturally bent. So when you are on a left circle, his neck will tend to be bent into the circle. His haunches might actually be drifting to the outside, but his front end will feel like he is bent around your leg.

There will also be a tendency for your horse to make smaller circles to the side he is naturally bent in.

Sounds familiar? If so, you're not alone. Most horses start life with a stronger side and a weaker side, and if left unchecked, that crookedness can maintain itself or even become more pronounced through riding. So it falls to the rider to become educated and sensitive enough to feel the crookedness – and then correct it over time. As with all other skills, if the horse is ridden in a manner that encourages suppleness and flexion, the horse will overcome the crookedness.

The rider, too, has a significant role in the process. For if the rider just follows the horse's movements, she will also be riding in a way that points her core to the wall, travelling with a crooked seat and imbalanced posture.

What is the shoulder-fore?

Although we often hear about the shoulder-in, we tend to overlook the shoulder-fore as a less worthy exercise. This is far from the truth. The shoulder-fore is easier to learn for both horse and rider and sets them on their way to becoming straighter and more supple.

The shoulder-fore is a movement that positions the horse's shoulders slightly to the inside of the hips. The way you know the horse is "in" shoulder-fore is by looking at the horse's footfalls. Simply put, the horse that has hind footsteps falling into front footsteps is straight. The horse that has the front footsteps landing slightly to the inside of the horse's hind footsteps is travelling in shoulder-fore.

Roya demonstrating a shoulder-fore on the right lead at the canter. Her front legs are slightly to the inside of the hind legs. This enables her to track straight, whether on or off the rail.

25

The shoulder-fore requires the horse to "articulate" more with the joints in the hind end, encourages a deeper stride length, and helps the horse balance better, allowing the energy to come over the topline and release the muscles over the back. It is a movement that should be in your riding vocabulary from the beginning to the end of the ride.

How to shoulder-fore:

1. Negotiate a turn or corner in the same manner as usual. Position your body on the bend to the inside, with your seat weighted slightly to the inside, inside leg at the girth, outside leg behind the girth and rein aids following your shoulders toward the turn.

2. Then come out of the turn.

3. But keep the horse on the same mild bend, going straight on the rail.

4. Feel for the horse's shoulders. They should feel slightly off-set to the inside.

At this point, the novice horse tends to want to fall into the middle of the ring, coming off the rail. It is the job of your inside leg, seat bone and rein to keep the horse on the line.

Your outside rein can also help to keep the straightness by half-halting to counter the horse's momentum toward the inside. It can also keep the neck fairly straight.

Get a friend to monitor your horse's foot falls and let you know about the angle of the horse's body. She should tell you when you have it right so that you can memorize what it feels like to have straightness in your horse's movements.

Shoulder-fore everywhere!

When you get good at it on the rail, try it off the rail. If you go straight up the ring on the quarter line, you will have enough room to your outside so that you have to really use your outside aids to help maintain the shoulder fore, but not so far that you can't use the rail as a reference point to see and feel the position of the shoulders.

Then try it on center line. It gets harder to feel the angle when there is no wall to gauge your position with. But eventually, you should be able to actually *feel* the angle of the horse's body regardless of whether or not you have a wall to refer to.

For more shoulder-fore fun, start up the center line with a right shoulder-fore, then as you cross X, switch to a left shoulder-fore.

Finally, give it a try on a circle. At this point, you should be able to identify the shoulder position on a bend. So when you feel that your horse is pointing his shoulders to the outside of the circle, be a responsible rider and bring those shoulders into the shoulder-fore position, even while you are travelling on a bend around the circle.

Results

See what your horse thinks about it. If you get a snort, be happy! If you get a softening of the neck and jaw to the inside, be thrilled. And if you get bouncy-bouncy, rolling gaits (do this in walk, trot and canter) and the feeling that you are spending more time in the air than on the ground, then celebrate!

For helping the horse to release tension, swing through the back, stay straight and energize is the goal of all riding!

*P.S. All the above is also equally relevant to the shoulder-in. But that can be a topic for another time.

35   Two Secrets to Easing Your Horse Into Suppleness

All riding disciplines value a horse that demonstrates suppleness while elegantly transitioning through his paces, floating weightlessly with pleasant engagement and enthusiasm. But many of us find that our horses feel more like rigid cardboard. Instead of bending seamlessly left then right, we find ourselves in a never ending tug-of-war against a braced jaw, poll, neck, back and hind end.

So precisely because we do not want to hurt the horse, we do nothing.

Instead, we become passive riders, not interfering with the horse but also not helping him achieve a healthier weight carriage. He travels with a stiff gait, crooked and hollow and eventually works his way into lameness – not because of what we did, but because of what we did *not* do.

Cyrus is practicing a walk pirouette to develop lateral suppleness.

We eventually learn that just hanging on and letting the horse travel incorrectly is not the solution. On the other hand, we don't want to push, pull and pretzel the horse into a fake shape that falls apart at a moment's notice anyway.

How can we find the happy medium?

Recently, I learned all over again about suppleness not through riding but through yoga and "listening" to the responses of my own body. Sometimes, there is no bigger lesson learned than through a personal first-hand experience.

To find suppleness in your own body, try practicing yoga. Or any martial arts, or dance or gymnastics.

Or choose another physical activity that you enjoy.

Then take notes.

Learn about how you can become more supple in your body. As you move through the stretching and bending routines, you will soon realize that you won't be able to force your body into looseness! In fact, the harder you try, the more tense your body will become. Instead, you will have to just go through the movements until your body can release through the muscles, tendons and ligaments. But this will take time.

The next time you go to yoga (or your activity of choice), your body will be more supple just on its own. You won't have to force or crunch – the muscles, tendons and ligaments will simply be more giving and "loose."

The same can be said for the horse.

The quickest way to suppleness in the horse is through regular practice and steadfast patience.

First: Practice

Practice is the first step toward suppleness. In riding, this translates to working on specific exercises that encourage the horse to move with more fluidity and grace. This means that rather than doing nothing, or just hanging on during the ride, we need to set up situations that promote release of the muscles.

Even if your horse feels like he simply can't soften or supple, work on getting him to release his topline. Ask for more impulsion. Try some stretches, work on bends. See if you can "accordion" the horse a few times, at the walk, trot and maybe even at the canter.

If your horse feels too tight to really respond, ease up on your aids a bit. But still ask and continue setting up the situations. Bend left, turn left. Bend right, turn right. Keep the turns soft and large but still try to get a mild bend from the horse.

Remember that the idea isn't to crank him into a frame. Rather, you want to invite him into softness through the body. This is something that cannot be forced. Position the horse and then soften the aids. See if you can loosen him up in the meantime.

Second: Patience

If you don't see instant results, don't get too disappointed. Understand that the stiffness you feel is deep within the horse's body and it might take several rides before he can loosen enough to respond to your expectations.

Patiently use your aids but don't rush him. Wait for him especially if you notice increased tension in response to your aids. Don't get stronger. Don't become frantic. Just ask and wait.

If the tension persists, finish the ride on a calm note and call it a day.

Try again the next ride. Work toward small improvements each day. You might be surprised to feel a more supple horse just like that!

36　How to "Flow" From the Trot to the Walk

Just pull back on the reins and the horse will stop trotting. But there are a lot of small details in there that might be overlooked. For example, you might notice the rider yanking back and the horse's mouth opening wide.

You might be able to see the neck come up in an upside-down arch, and the back drop into a hammock-like position.

The most obvious problem that can be visibly identified is the hind legs. When the transition is problematic, the hind legs literally get left behind. The striding is short and the legs seem to be stuck together, causing an imbalance that then gets transmitted to the front end. The horse "falls to the forehand".

Although we rely on our hands too much and initiate all movements from the horse's mouth, there are many alternate aids we can go to, especially for a downward transition. Here are three steps to develop a balanced trot-walk transition with minimal rein pressure:

Preparing for the walk transition with a half-halt.

1. Half-Halt

Several steps before you want to do the downward transition, do three of four half-halts. IN the rhythm of the trot, use a light leg aid to encourage the horse to reach further underneath the body with his hind legs. Then go like this: half-halt, half-halt, half-halt.

The half-halt comes mainly from your back and seat, followed by light squeezes from your already closed hands. Resist with your lower back and seat against the trot movement. If you are posting in your trot, do the resisting when on the sitting phase.

2. Walk With Your Seat

Immediately after the half-halt, sit into the walk. Your seat should not only resist any more trot movement, but also change its rhythm to a walk rhythm. Once your horse knows to expect the change in your seat, he will easily switch his legs to a walk when he feels the walk from your seat. At this point, if you think using a voice cue would be beneficial, use a low, calming tone to "walk". At some point, though, you want to see if your horse is responding to your riding aids rather than just the voice.

3. Follow Through

If he still goes through your seat and half-halt aids, momentarily close your legs and knees to support your resisting back. Push down into your stirrups.

As a last resort, use the reins. But keep in mind that...
Every pull backwards on the reins prevents the horse's hind legs from reaching underneath the body.

But there *is* more to it.

The ideal transition should simply and easily flow from one gait to the other.

4. Just One More Thing...

Many horses tend to "flop" into the downward transition. Some horses fall heavily to the forehand and eventually change gaits; others simply like to quit. Those are the horses that lurch into the walk, with little effort put into supporting their weight from the hind end.

Ideally, the energy should continue at the same level, irrespective of the gait. So whether the horse is trotting or walking, there should be the same amount of fluidity to the movement.

To ensure continued movement, don't stop your seat when the horse breaks to the walk. Add enough leg aid to keep the energy flowing forward. Instead, without skipping a beat, swing your seat from the trot into the walk, within the movement of one horse stride. Go with the same commitment and flow as the trot.

Encourage with your leg aids if needed, and expect your horse to switch just as easily from the trot to the walk. Don't give up if you can't get it right away. Instead, practice the "flow" at every opportunity and soon enough, you'll notice that your horse isn't getting stuck in his downward transitions. Then, be sure to pat him to thank him for his efforts!

37   What To Do When the Half-Halt Just Won't Do

It has probably happened to you too many times to mention: Coming to a turn, you asked for a half-halt.

Preparing for a transition, you wanted a soft rebalancing before the new gait.

Half-way around the circle, you half-halted in order to prevent your horse from leaning in or out.

You felt your horse stiffen and you used a half-halt to ask him to loosen once again.

Maybe all you wanted to do was get your horse's attention before the next transition.

…and NOTHING HAPPENED!

Your horse did not understand.

He tensed his head and neck and went against your half-halt. He hollowed his back and ran faster and faster (or conversely, shuffled along slower and slower).

Maybe he flat out ignored you!

In the end, it doesn't really matter *why* the half-halt did not "go through". There could be a thousand and one reasons why! The fact is, it did not work.

What Not To Do

Push the horse so he gets tighter/faster/stronger and works against your aids.

Do more of the same and expect different results.

Get offended by his personal vendetta against you!

Give up.

Looking Closer

Balance does not happen magically on its own. When you watch a gorgeous horse and rider combination apparently floating along weightlessly, reading each other's minds, recognize that they are continually balancing and *re*balancing gait to gait, stride to stride and moment to moment.

The idea is to help the horse keep his weight on the hind end (rather than fall to the forehand) before, during and after transitions. Because a half-halt is not a slowing down aid, the horse should ideally keep up his energy and impulsion while simultaneously shifting his balance off his forehand. When a horse has difficulty rebalancing in movement (for whatever reason), he simply can't help you in that moment. So you have to find another way to explain that he should take his weight to the hind end.

What To Do

I like to think of it as a "full" half-halt. Not as in a full halt. Far from it. Instead of trying the half-halt over and over, just follow through until the horse does a full transition down from the gait you were at. If you were in canter, go to trot. If you were in trot, go to walk. If you were already in walk, go to an under-power walk (not halt, obviously).

Wait at the slower gait until you get what you want. Perhaps you needed a shoulder out of the way. Maybe you wanted a rounder body outline.

Maybe you were asking for the hind legs to reach deeper underneath the body. In all those cases, do a full downward transition, work at the more controlled (= balanced) gait, get what you wanted, and then *go right back to what you were doing.*

Don't Forget!

The one downfall to this technique is that many riders fall into the "slower is better" rut. Keep in mind that you are not exactly trying to slow the horse down. You do not want to lose the energy or impulsion you already have.

Rather, you are helping him to *balance* better before you increase the difficulty at a higher gait. One thing you want to avoid is to do a downward transition and stay there. As soon as you feel the horse has balanced and responded to your aid, go back to your original task.

Immediately switch back to canter, if that was the gait you were working at. Then do the same lesson you were doing, ask with a half-halt, and see what happens. Your horse might respond quite nicely. You will say "yes" and go to the next thing.

Your horse might not respond at all. In this case, you should do another "full half-halt". You might need to do it a few times in a row until your horse is better able to work from his haunches.

One time, after several repetitions of "full half-halt", try the half-halt again. It just might happen that your horse has an easier time sitting down and balancing to the hind end.
If you have a softer, more responsive horse, you know you are on the right track.

If your horse feels more supple and loose over the topline, you know you are getting closer.

If your horse catapults you out of your tack with heartfelt snorts, you know you've got the ticket!

38   Why a Halt is Not a Vacation

Admit it! You've done it, I've done it, and until we really blueprint the right "feel" into our body, we'll all continue to do it more often than not.

What Happens After You Halt Your Horse?

Do you sit back and relax? Adjust your seat position, step into one and then the other stirrup, adjust your reins? Do you take a look around, think about where you have to go after the barn and say hi to a passing friend?

Does your horse brace against your aids, stop with his hind legs camped out, hollow back and giraffe neck?

Or maybe he closes his eyes, licks his lips, and <gasp> rests a hind leg.

I'm exaggerating, but you know what I mean. Essentially, most of us turn off when we stop riding. The seat goes soft, the legs come off the horse, and we drop the reins. It's not surprising then that the horse reflects our inactivity.

Vacation Time?

The first thing we need to understand is that when we halt, we should not be going on a mental or physical vacation. Halting is not about stopping everything. It should not be a relaxation – although it could be a "regrouping" or a "collection" of the thoughts and aids.

Neither you nor your horse should feel like you can go on a mini-vacation when you halt. If you do, you will have a difficult time re-establishing everything from your aids, to your horse's energy level, your frame of mind and your two-way communication.

Three Components of A Halt

Similar to other transitions, the halt can be broken down into at least three phases:

1. The Preparation

The preparation phase might take longer or shorter depending on your horse. Horses who have a stronger affinity for halting (!) won't need as long of a heads-up. Regardless, you should be preparing for the halt several strides before the actual halt, even if only mentally. Where will the halt happen? How engaged is the horse as he is going into the halt?

You will often need to put an extra bit of "oomph" coming into the halt so that the horse will halt from the hind end. This means that you should use leg and seat to increase impulsion through the last few strides before asking for the halt. Initially, your halt aids might require a stronger rein contact but that should not be your goal.

You want a nice, balanced halt coming out of a sequence of half-halts. The only thing your reins should be doing is keeping the horse straight and helping using the half-halts. As time goes on, you want to teach your horse to respond to your seat aids so that once your seat stops, the horse stops. It's amazing when it finally happens.

2. The Action

If you're like me, you'll be surprised to think of the halt as an "action". But we must think of it as an active movement if we want to have a round, well-balanced halt.

The horse should be standing evenly on all four legs, with the legs "square" underneath him like the legs of a table. You want to work toward having all four legs engaged in the halt, and the horse standing quietly but ready to go at a moment's notice.

This is why you can't go on vacation yourself. You have to stay engaged through your legs and seat as well.

3. The Follow-Through

Wait! Don't pack it in yet!

You can't be done when you halt. During the transition to the halt, you have to already be thinking about what is going to come next. *After* you've halted, prepare for the next topic. Don't think about it after the legs have stopped. Have it all planned ahead of time so once you've achieved the halt, you can start getting ready for the next movement. Whether it's a walk, trot or canter, you will need to prepare your legs and seat for what is to come.

Cyrus in the moment he steps forward out of the halt.

What comes after the halt is almost as important as the halt itself. If the horse is well-balanced in the halt, the next transition will be smooth, fluid and easy to achieve. The horse will be able to keep his balance, engagement and roundness through the transition to the next movement.

Long Term

If you practice the three-step halt, soon enough, your body will become used to the prep, the stop and the next steps. In time, you won't even have to think of it as a three-step process, and your body will just do the "oomph"/prep/half-halt/halt/go on its own.

You'll know you're on the right track if your halts become smoother, quicker and more accurate, and with next to no fuss. Your transitions down to the halt and up to the next gait will be precise, energetic and enthusiastic.

39   Done With Going Round and Round on the Rail? Try the "10/5" Challenge!

Do you ever get stuck in the same rut ride after ride? It is true that finding a routine is a good idea because it gives you and your horse a sense of structure that you can build upon over time.

But there are times when you want to spice things up before you pack it up!

Use the 10/5 Challenge when:
- you're both done with that 50th loop around the rail and want to do something completely "off the wall" (pun intended!)
- you feel that everything went right in the ride and there's still more left in you and your horse for a bang-up last effort
- you want to get the kinks out and release tension in you and your horse

- you want to develop hind end engagement and larger hind end strides
- your horse is feeling a little lethargic and "uninspired"
- your horse is too pumped up and needs to put his energy somewhere
- you want to fine-tune your aids and transitions
- you want to play a little with a "last dance" before you're done for the day

In any case, this exercise will help both you and your horse work out of your tightness. It encourages your horse to loosen over the topline, work out his balance and engagement, and in general, become better able to work through any transition.

The 10/5 Challenge

The idea is pretty simple. You want to do 10 strides of one thing and then 5 strides of something else.

For example:
- 10 strides canter/5 strides trot
- 10 strides left and 5 strides right
- 10 strides canter/5 strides walk
- 10 strides leg yield/5 strides shoulder-in

There really are an infinite of variations you can use.
But I love the first one the most, especially for beginner to intermediate horse and riders, so let's break that one down more for an example.

1. Canter

Go into a canter. Make sure you have a "decent" canter to start – encourage your horse onward if at all possible.

2. Count strides.

The idea is to hit the transition on that 10 mark, and be absolutely picky about changing gaits in the 10th stride.

3. Transition to trot.

You might have to really prepare for this transition at first. Chances are, your horse will not be expecting a downward transition so soon, so be ready to reinforce your asking aids as soon as you can. The idea is to stay in that 10 stride number. So be picky.

4. Transition to canter.

But watch out! Don't "sit" on your laurels! Those 5 strides are over before you know it, and you have got to get back into the canter on the fifth trot stride!

And there is the real challenge. This exercise requires you to be sharp, accurate and physically in sync with your horse. The quickness of the transitions will jolt you into a higher level of accuracy and timing. The physicality of the transitions will have you both huffing and puffing in no time. Just remember to keep breathing! You might solicit a nice body-shaking snort from your horse in the process. That is a good sign.

5. Do it again!

The first time is probably going to be the easiest for a while. The next bunch of tries will really highlight the areas that need to come together for a better transition. As your horse starts to realize that there will be more and more transitions, he may go through some tension and resistance before he can gather up his strength and balance to be able to smoothly make so many transitions.

You might discover a few issues as well! Initially, the transitions come up very quickly. You might feel overwhelmed and thrown off balance a bit. Keep at it. If you find yourself not making the 10 strides, do 12. But aim for 10. Figure out how to adjust your timing for the transitions. You might have to do the "ask" for both the upward and downward several strides before.

Practice. Stick with the program 10, 20 times even if things don't go well. You will get better at it and your horse will become more balanced. Things will start falling together. The next time you try this, you might discover that the horse has an easier time with the transitions and responds more smoothly and efficiently to the aids.

Of all the exercises I've used, I'd recommend this one the most for anyone to try at any level. It works well with an advanced horse/rider combination as well as for the beginner rider or horse.

You can make it a very basic exercise of one simple transition or complicate it as much as you would like. If the canter/trot is too simple, move onto something that challenges both you and your horse. Do the transitions while you change directions. Change leads and then break to the trot. The variations are limitless!

40   Twenty-Three Ways to Solve the Riding Problem

Got a horseback riding problem? Here are 23 ways to solve it!

23 WAYS TO SOLVE THE RIDING PROBLEM
Buy a new saddle.
Buy a saddle pad.
Change the bit. Change your coach.
Add a "gimmick" piece of equipment.
Try your friend's best whip.
SHUT THE HORSE'S MOUTH WITH A DROP/FLASH/FIGURE-EIGHT/CRANK (ETC.) NOSEBAND
Always ride with your friends. change your coach again.
Always ride alone.
DON'T RIDE INTO THE SPOOKY CORNER.
Avoid upsetting the horse.
GET MAD AT THE HORSE.
GIVE THE HORSE TREATS. Reward the horse.
DON'T GIVE THE HORSE TREATS!
CHANGE THE HORSE'S FEED PROGRAM. Call the vet.
Change the barn. CHANGE YOUR HORSE'S FARRIER.
Call the chiropractor. CALL THE ANIMAL COMMUNICATOR.
CHANGE THE HORSE!

Admit it – you've tried at least a handful of these in your time! (So have I... trust me, I have the T-shirt for many of these "solutions"!)

I'm also quite sure you can think of many other ways to solve the problem. The message here is not that you *shouldn't* try some of the strategies above.

Of course we should make sure that the equipment fits the horse and there is no underlying physical problem. We should know if our horse prefers one bit over another.

Without a doubt, you might need the help of a friend or a professional throughout the course of your ownership of the horse.

But in the midst of fiddling with the small things, we end up missing out on the bigger picture:

changing ourselves.

The unfortunate part of having to develop our skills is that it takes time. The learning process is slow, strewn with mistakes and less-than-perfects, and at times, even discouraging.

In order to make a true change, we have to dig deep and change our very way of interacting with the horse. This is not the stuff that happens in a day or two. Forget instant gratification and prepare to stay for the long haul.

We have to persevere, make mistakes, try something new. We must step out of our comfort zones and use new muscles – physically and mentally.

Aside from the physical discomfort, we have to develop our internal characteristics. We learn to let things go and to forgive both our horse and ourselves. We become more humble, less demanding and more persistent. We learn all about developmental stages, both within ourselves as well as our horses.

And perhaps most importantly, we discover what it feels like to stay the course and really struggle with something difficult, seeing our way through the problems to finally finding the solutions.

Only then do we become empowered in the understanding that if we can "find" the change we need within ourselves, the horse will reward us with a positive response.

And by that time, we might be startled to realize that the problem no longer exists!

41   Finding Your Horse's "Happy Place"

Before we discuss what to do, first, let's explore how to prevent the horse from being his best – in riding as well as in general health and contentment.

Withdraw regular "creature" comforts.

Don't provide shelter and blanketing; don't worry if he gets cold or shivers or overheats – for horses should be out in all elements as they are "creatures of the wild". Ignore the effects of the elements. Above all, pay no attention to tight backs and any signs of physical discomfort.

Don't provide nutritional feed and definitely not at regular time intervals.

Worry not about tight flanks, the signs of hunger (pacing, anxiety, pawing) or the lone horse that is regularly kicked off the hay in the field. Ignore any signs of ulcers/

malnutrition/lack of worming. Feed only when you have the time – the horses won't die without hay over the course of several hours! Loss of weight and condition means nothing with regards to the riding capacity of the horse.

Ignore tack and physical discomforts.

Any saddle is fine – get the cheapest one you can find, especially those "all in one" kits that are on sale for a price that even you can't believe! Use any girth/cinch you can find – if there is a girth gall, just slap on some ointment. Don't worry too much about the length and angles of the hooves – long, low toes might cause your horse to trip a little, but just kick the horse on when that happens.

Avoid a consistent exercise routine.

Life is busy – ride only when you have nothing better to do. Ride at different times on the days you do ride and certainly don't concern yourself with developing a training routine for your warm-up and cool-down.

Ride the same way over and over again...

... especially if you are running into problems. Repeat your aids and make them stronger until at some point, the horse finally gives in.

It's too much trouble to try something new or improve your own riding skills. If you never "get through" to the horse, or if he becomes too dangerous to ride, sell him. Buy another one with a higher tolerance for your riding techniques.

Don't bother taking riding lessons.

Once you know how to stay on and steer and stop, the sky is the limit! Believe in the old adage, "What you don't know won't hurt you." Riding lessons are expensive and only serve to confuse and irritate.

Don't use half-halts.

Ignore your horse's complaints about being off-balance. Some horses tolerate being on the forehand better than others; buy those and ride them until they go lame. If the horse is repeatedly lame, sell him off and buy another.

Be inconsistent with your aids.

Keep the horse guessing at all times. Instead of learning to work with the horse, make him be the only active partner. Keep changing things up so that he doesn't know when he is right or wrong, and avoid putting in the hard work it takes to develop a kind hand and an informed seat.

Don't listen to your horse.

Do your best to ignore your horse's body language, especially if the "feedback" is negative. Also avoid the input of other people who might be concerned for your horse's welfare.

Happy Place, Anyone?

Now let's look at alternatives to the above negatives. Did you know that through riding, you can help your horse achieve a happy, content outlook on life? Sounds ridiculously far-fetched? Too good to be true?

There are ways that we can find the "happy place" we all so desire for our horses. Try a few of these riding tips and see the results you get from your horse.

The outside of the horse mirrors his internal state.

Horses don't lie. Without a doubt, you can clearly "read" how the horse feels just by watching him being ridden (or riding him yourself – then, you get even more feedback).

Essentially, the horse's "outline" tells you his state of mind. Of course, you need to know what to look for, but once you can identify the communication signs, you will know exactly what is going on inside the mind of the horse.

A round, forward-moving, enthusiastic horse is in his happy place. His ears will be lightly forward (occasionally flicking back and forth on and off his rider) and he will be moving with expression. He looks like he is enjoying what he is doing, and moving on his own initiative.

In contrast, the unhappy horse is reluctant, sluggish, ears back (not necessarily pinned), and looking like the movement is belabored. The strides are short, the back is hollow and the horse is not "using" himself well enough to be comfortable under the rider. He will have a tendency to be on the forehand, and inconsistently responsive.

Have a consistent "yes" and "no".

Cyrus' happy place face!

Horses are just like the rest of us: they thrive on positive feedback. In establishing your riding parameters, you must communicate "yes" and "no" regularly and consistently. In fact, you might need to communicate one or the other message as quickly as stride to stride! If you communicate less frequently, you will not be helping the horse and he may end up wondering – what am I doing wrong?

Many riders use a low, soft "goooood" voice aid to reinforce the correct response from the horse, however, the same effect can be gained by saying "yes" through the *body*. If you can find a "yes" answer physically (release of your joints, following through the seat versus resisting, or allowing through all your aids), you can communicate the "yes" message faster than you can say it.

And this is the way your horse can find his happy place – because he knows where he stands and gets regular and consistent feedback quickly enough to be able to respond to it and find his place of comfort.

Listen for the snort and feel for the licking and chewing.

There is no more obvious sign of the horse in his happy place other than the snort. A little snort is a good sign, a loud, wet, heart-felt series of snorts that rock you out of the saddle is ideal! (Have a snorting contest with your riding partner: who can be the first to get a snort out of their horse? Who can get the most snorts out of their horse?!)

In general, after the snort session, you will find the horse licking and chewing like he just ate something exquisite and tasty – and yes, the horse can do all the above even while trotting and cantering. The final sign of contentment is the saliva that coats around the lips of the horse. A dry mouth usually denotes discomfort or stress of some sort; drool is a key indicator of "happy place" heaven!

Do something fun!

When the "learning" part of your session is over, or if you want to take a brief reprieve after a difficult stretch of work, let the horse do something he likes. One horse might enjoy a stretchy trot; another prefers a lengthen; still another gets a kick (not literally!) out of a flying change! Every horse has one or more favourite exercises – listen carefully to your horse to identify his preference, and then use that movement as a moment of celebration!

Look for any excuse to celebrate!

Everyone loves a celebration! Don't leave your horse out – invite him to celebrate with you at every opportunity; in fact, look for excuses to celebrate! Did he just struggle through a particularly difficult movement? Celebrate! Did he lick and chew and release his topline for the first time in the ride?

Celebrate!

I'm sure you're starting to get the idea. Let me know if you gave any of these tips a try, or if you have any other "happy place" tips you can share. Happy riding!

* The assumption is that all the other bare necessities (feed, shelter, etc.) as discussed above have already been met.*

42   Dressage As A Healing Tool

At its essence, the French term, *dressage*, means "training". In effect, all we do when we ride "dressage", is develop a better training regimen for both ourselves and our horses. Regardless of discipline, solid basic training is what every movement is based upon.

Even at its most basic level (or perhaps, especially at the most basic levels), dressage holds a value to horses of all disciplines.

Done well, it presents opportunity for you to analyze your horse's way of going, strengthening weaknesses and evening out imbalances in movement.

Done well, it provides you opportunity to develop your basic riding skills, strengthening weaknesses and evening out imbalances in your aids. Because both are critical to your horse's success in performance, and your success as a rider. What do dressage exercises do for the horse?

Stretching/Releasing/Bending/Strengthening

If riding were a language (which in fact, it is), then the alphabet would be based on the above qualities of movement. The foundation for all movements begin with the horse's ability to stretch, release, bend and be strong.

All four qualities combine to allow the horse to move in a way that keeps him sound and physically functional for years to come. If any one component is missing, then the horse runs the risk of joint/muscle/tendon injury.

Stretching

There are two ways a horse can stretch – longitudinally (over the topline), and laterally (side to side). The former is usually the first to be accomplished well and the latter improves along with the topline as that develops. As a young horse learns to stretch, the muscles have an easier time releasing and working in tandem.

Releasing (Suppling)

Some people refer to muscle release as "relaxation" – as in, the horse should relax while cantering. However, a horse cannot truly relax in movement – he must "release" his muscles instead.

You will know that your horse released his muscles by how the movement feels: fluid, ground-covering, lightweight and sometimes even bouncy. Your horse's expression might change – from tense ears to soft and floppy, from almost no breathing sounds to snorts and deep grunts. You know you are in true suppleness when the movements feel effortless.

Stiffness and tension are the opposites to a release. Horses ridden with tight muscling develop mystery lamenesses and other ailments over the long term. All riding exercises should be aimed toward improving the horse's ability to release the muscles through particular exercises and limit stiffness and tension as much as possible.

Bending

Increased ability to stretch and release over the topline will invariably lead to better bending. All horses have a preferred side, much like humans have a dominant hand. Better bending will lead to better evenness in the left and right body. The horse will develop his ability to bear weight more evenly on both hind legs, and therefore stretch through both sides in an easier manner.

Strength

You might be amazed at the horse's development once the muscles work together instead of against each other. First of all, the horse's muscling will change visibly. You might notice a top line musculature where there was none before. You might notice a squaring of the rump when viewed from behind.

There might also be a delightful groove developing over the horse's back over the spine, a sure indication of supple muscles working underneath the saddle. But the clincher is that the horse becomes capable of doing the movements (in whatever discipline) easier, slower and with more control.

The Healthy Horse

Regardless of our disciplines, we want horses to live long and thrive in their work until old age. Adding dressage exercises regularly into your routine workouts will always reap benefits in several areas at once.

When combined, the above components of riding will result in the horse's increased capacity for correct weight-bearing. And more than anything, improving the horse's ability to carry the rider's weight in a manner that not only prevents damage, but in fact *improves* the horse's health and well-being, is what all good riding should endeavor to produce.

43   Forty-Two Ways to Play, Learn and Grow With Your Horse

Horses give to us in countless ways. We play, learn and grow with them, making horseback riding not merely a sport (which it truly is, like no other), but so much more. Here are forty-two ways that you can interact with a horse!

Play

1. Give your horse a great grooming session and focus especially on his sweet spots!
2. Teach your horse to bow/lie down/count/"target"/hug.

3. See if you can get your horse to come to you – at walk then trot then canter!

4. Get your horse to leave you when you ask him to.

5. Do shoulder-in/travers/half-pass/medium!

6. Go for a strong and exhilarating gallop.

7. Go to a horse show just for the fun of it.

8. Hang out in the pasture.

9. Listen to the horses munching on their hay during a quiet moment at the barn.

10. Give your horse a good sniff!

11. Join a musical riding group.

12. Bake some homemade horsey treats.

13. Witness the grace and beauty of horses running in the pasture.

Learn

14. Figure out how to teach him how to respond to a pull on a lead rope.

15. Always keep safety first.

16. Learn the aids for specific movements.

17. Keep your horse (and yourself?) straight(er).

18. Develop better timing or your aids.

19. Lighten your aids and get the same or better responses.

20. Feel your way to doing "nothing" on horseback.

21. Study the biomechanics of equine movement.

22. Learn all about good equine nutrition and care.

23. Go to a show to meet goals and become better at what you do.

24. Use a better outside rein.

25. Ride mostly from <u>your seat</u>.

26. Show your horse the way to his "happy place" while riding.

27. Find true "forward".

Grow

28. Develop your confidence as you begin to believe that you can work in tandem with such a magnificent animal.

29. Be humble when things don't go your way.

30. See the bigger picture in the long run.

31. Understand that the horses rely entirely on your hard wok for their well-being – despite how much work it may be.

32. Develop your own consistency and stability of character.

33. Stay calm in tense situations.

34. Laugh at yourself or at your (lack of?) performance.

35. Become gracious in your successes.

36. Mature into a strong sense of security and self-sufficiency.

37. Be patient and wait for the horse (and yourself?) to develop.

38. Figure out that the path is just as important as the end goal.

39. Live in the moment. Revel in the simplicity of life.

40. Let go of instant gratification.

41. Develop empathy and compassion.

42. Become a horse listener!

The Front End

Although everything in riding starts from the hind end of the horse, the front end cannot be ignored. In fact, one might say that navigating the front of the horse might even be more of an art than the hind end.

It is obvious to even the newest newbie rider that controlling the front end of the horse is one of the most important aspects of riding a horse. Many an accident begins with the horse that, for whatever reason, does not stop his legs when necessary.

But as we become more adept at riding with our cores and through our bodies, we realize that after achieving a certain level of basic control, we can allow the front of the horse to develop in accordance with the hind end. The more weight carriage on the hind, the less you might need to do on the front.

So in a seemingly counterintuitive way, as we improve our

skills, we can "let the horse go" without letting him *go*. We learn, with increasingly subtler aids, to give, to loosen and to rebalance in order to recycle the horse's energy to his hind end, thereby relieving the front legs from the burden of the horse and rider's weight. Without the front aids, the concept and feel of "round" would elude even the most dedicated of riders. This is because even while we create energy from the active hind end, we must also contain and redistribute it to create an adequate balance for the rider-carrying horse.

So while it took me several years to develop an effective enough seat that usually encourages good activity and engagement from the horse's hind end, it has taken more than double the time to develop a kind, gentle but useful contact that guides the horse but allows the horse freedom in the front end.

In fact, I'd have to say that I'm still working on improving my coordination, suppleness and clarity of the rein aids. In a sense, I am not sure that I will be able to ever say that I'm done with learning about feel and contact. I think like anything worth pursuing, just when you think you know something, you discover that there is so much more for you to learn – even about the same subject!

And so my challenge to you is to start from where you are, and slowly but surely, ride, practice and take lessons. Develop a forward and round movement (in both your horse and yourself), and do what you can to keep your horse sound, happy and rideable into old age.

And remember to listen to your horse in the process. Because he will guide you as you walk, trot and canter along your path!

Connect with your horse

HorseListening.com

The Blog

Find us at www.HorseListening.com

Keep an eye out for Book 3 in the Horse Listening Collection!

Join us on Facebook and Twitter for daily articles that inspire, educate and share our love for the horse.

ABOUT THE AUTHOR

Kathy Farrokhzad has been involved in the equine industry for the past 20 years as a rider, boarder, horse owner, competitor, coach, trainer and breeder. Horse Listening symbolizes the path that has brought her to writing and riding, through a myriad of experiences that have enriched her life and provided her opportunity for growth.

With riding backgrounds encompassing western performance, endurance riding and competitive trail, natural horsemanship, and most prominently, dressage, Kathy has developed into a well-rounded and open-minded equestrian, always in search of more learning!

She considers her first book, Horse Listening – The Book: Stepping Forward to Effective Riding, *and now this second book in the series, to be one of her biggest accomplishments. The reception has been very encouraging!*

Thank you to those who have already read the books. There is now a third book in the works!

Do you wish your horseback riding lessons could come with a user manual? Do you feel that you could serve your horses better as a rider if you only know how and what to do? Would you like to be the rider that all horses dream of?

"Horse Listening: The Book" focuses specifically on riding as a means of improving the horse. Based on the popular blog, HorseListening.com, the exercises and ideas are purposely handpicked to help you develop your path to becoming an effective rider, not only for your own benefit, but also for your horse's long-term well-being. Special "In the Ring" sections give specific suggestions to try while riding.

Horse Listening – The Book

Buy the first book in the Horse Listening Collection at www. amazon.com

By following these simple, useful exercises, you will be able to develop a better understanding about:
- the rider's aids
- the use of the seat
- the half-halt
- accurate turns and circles
- transitions
- hind end engagement
- rein lameness

Made in the USA
Coppell, TX
15 January 2020

14561970R00134